Musical Starting Points

JEAN GILBERT

CATIONAL

WARD LOCK EDUCATIONAL CO. LTD.
1 CHRISTOPHER ROAD
EAST GRINSTEAD
SUSSEX RH19 3BT
UNITED KINGDOM

A MEMBER OF THE LING KEE GROUP
HONG KONG • SINGAPORE • LONDON • NEW YORK

First published - 1981
Reprinted – 1984, 1985, 1989, 1990, 1991, 1992 (twice)

ISBN 0-7062-4045-6

Printed in Hong Kong

Contents

Acknowledgments

The basic ideas and approaches outlined here are a continuation of those presented in *Musical Activities with Young Children* which was published by Ward Lock Educational in 1975. When that book went out of print I was asked to extend and develop the activities to cover an age range of 4+ to 8 years – roughly the three years of the Infant school with an overlap either end.

In writing *Musical Starting Points* I have concentrated on musical activities in the classroom and have considered their relation to other aspects of the curriculum. In my own classroom teaching of young children I have found that integrating music into the curriculum so that it becomes part of their daily learning allows more opportunity for all of them to become involved at their own level.

Like so many other teachers I have been influenced by the ideas of some of the great music educators, particularly those of John Curwen and of Carl Orff and Kodály who followed and developed Curwen's principles in different ways. I have also been influenced by the BBC's school radio and television music programmes which have been a continual source of stimulating ideas. I acknowledge my indebtedness to all these sources.

I would like to thank my friends and colleagues who have read the manuscript of this book and given their comments as practising teachers. I am particularly indebted to Robina Gilbert for her continual help and encouragement in the preparation of the script and to Claudia Clarke, the Music Adviser of the London Borough of Haringey, for her most valuable comments on the manuscript. She has always been ready to listen and advise whenever I have approached her in connection with my work in music education.

The author and publishers would like to thank the following for their permission to reproduce copyright material: William Collins, Sons & Company Ltd for 'Creation' by Graeme Turner from *Stuff and Nonsense*; Evans Brothers Ltd for 'Noises in the Night' by Lilian McCrae from *Come Follow Me*; David Evans for 'Wiggley Woo' from *Sing-a-Song One* published by Thomas Nelson & Sons Ltd; Barbara Ireson for 'The Grocers' from *Rhyme Time* published by Hamlyn; Martin Lee for 'Ten Miles from Home' from *Singing Fun* published by George Harrap & Company Ltd; 'Rain Sizes' by John Ciardi from *The Reason for the Pelican* © J. B. Lippincott Company; Alan Lomax for 'The Little Pig' from *American Ballads and Folk Songs* by John A. and Alan Lomax published by Macmillan Publishing Company Inc; the Literary Trustees of Walter de la Mare and The Society of Authors as their representative for 'Someone' by Walter de la Mare; 'Wind Song' from Lilian Moore, *I Feel the Same Way* Copyright © 1967 by Lilian Moore (New York: Atheneum, 1967) Reprinted with the permission of Atheneum Publishers; 'The Elephants' and 'Shortnin' Bread' are reproduced from *More Songs for Music Time* published by Oxford University Press; 'Down in the Forest' by Anne Mendoza and 'The Postman' by Edward Hughes are reproduced by permission of Novello & Company Ltd; Pitman Books Ltd for 'The Music Makers' and 'Rain, Hail, Snow' from *Listen to the Band* by M. Cobby and I. M. Warner; Stainer & Bell Ltd for 'Five Little Field Mice' by Cynthia Raza from *Mungo Mouse*; 'Floating Down the River' from *Handy Play Party Book* published by World Around Songs, Burnsville, NC 28714, USA.

Every effort has been made to trace owners of copyright material, but in some cases this has not proved possible. The publishers would be glad to hear from any further copyright owners of material reproduced in *Musical Starting Points with Young Children*.

Introduction

All too often music in the primary school is held to be the province of the specialist and the teaching of it is regarded as a rare skill only to be undertaken by those with a thorough music training. Whilst a good music specialist is an asset to any school, especially if she works closely with the class teacher, there are very few of them in the primary field, with the result that music is often left out completely or included only when it is required for a special occasion.

I take the view that music should be an integral part of the school curriculum of every young child, not simply something to be introduced for Christmas or the Harvest Festival. Music plays an important role in everyday life: we hear it on radio and television, in the supermarket and in churches; we dance to it, relax with it, are refreshed by it. We seem to need it; in fact it is difficult to imagine a society without some form of music. Such an essential need would justify its inclusion in any school curriculum. Sadly it is the one area that is most often neglected, usually because it is equated with a high level of musicianship on the part of the teacher. But, as teachers, we provide for art and craft whether or not we can paint, weave or make clay pots; what we don't know about these skills we learn from courses, from other people, and we try things out first. I believe that an enthusiastic class teacher, especially if she is willing to acquire some basic skills, can similarly provide a wide variety of simple activities in music, and that both she and the children can gain many benefits from the richer curriculum that will result.

Musical activities can complement and extend other areas of classroom work, especially language – as outlined in the section on singing, and maths – through rhythm work, number rhymes and the use of flashcards in percussion groups. I have also found that these activities offer an invaluable variety when planning for a balanced day. They can give great pleasure to the children and, although I would stress enjoyment as one of the main aims in introducing these activities, there are other benefits in the contributions that they can make to the physical, social, intellectual, emotional and aesthetic areas of child growth. Group music making, for instance, requires self-discipline;

exploring sound and responding to music can help to develop self-expression; playing percussion aids rhythmic development and muscular co-ordination, and auditory perception and discrimination are heightened through all the listening involved.

The aim of this book is to provide a resource for the class teacher who wishes to include music in her classroom scheme. It suggests a number of starting points and how they might be developed. Although they do not represent a scheme in music, they do cover most of the activities that can be introduced into the classroom. Movement is included where it is integral to classroom activities, although it is such an important aspect of child development that full coverage would require a book in itself. There are many useful books available on this subject, some of which are mentioned in the Bibliography.

This book is only a starter. There are many methods of teaching music in schools, and for those who are interested, the Appendix gives details of some well-known approaches, together with addresses to contact for further information. Curwen, Kodály and Orff, among others, provide excellent structured schemes and courses are sometimes available to teachers for training in these methods. Ask your music adviser for advice and relevant details.

HOW TO BEGIN

Start by selecting a musical activity that you can do and enjoy with your children and gradually extend the range according to the particular age group, background and abilities of your children (see page 8 for suggestions). I do not wish to infer that musical education should be haphazard, rather that the underlying aim of enjoyment should be borne in mind. If the advice and guidance of a specialist teacher is available, then the ideal situation of working within a planned structure for the school as a whole can be attained. Even without such a skilled co-ordinator, it is possible to agree upon approaches to musical activities through staff meetings, as with other areas of the curriculum.

	Nursery, Reception, Young Infants (age 4–6 years approx.)	Upper Infants, Lower Juniors (age 6–8 years approx.)
Listening Activities	Simple listening games involving single and easily contrasted sounds.	Extension of listening games involving greater numbers of similar sounds, and introduction of tuned instruments.
	Listening to 'live' music and very short extracts of recorded music linked with movement, etc.	More specific listening – own and friends' performances, longer extracts of recorded music.
Singing	Nursery rhymes, finger plays, singing games – plenty of easy repetitive verse-and-chorus songs.	Include more traditional folk songs, songs for topic work and with slightly more 'content'.
	Unaccompanied singing.	Very simple piano/guitar or children's own accompaniment on tuned percussion.
Percussion	'Body sounds' with singing games and action songs. Instruments and sound makers for simple chorus and action songs – percussion group training.	More complicated use of body sounds. More specific use of instruments.
Tuned Instruments	General handling of these instruments. Limited use with songs. Very simple ostinati.	Longer ostinati.
	Playing simple 'snippets' or tunes with 2–3 notes.	Playing longer tune snippets and trying a complete tune.
Exploring Sound	Exploring sound and introduction to very simple sound pictures.	More complicated group sound pictures.
Finding Out	Sound in the environment. Simple experiments.	More purposeful investigation of sound; introduction of simple physics underlying sound experiments.

I LISTENING

One of the most important skills a young child needs to develop is that of listening; it is absolutely vital if he is to benefit from any of the learning situations we provide for him and we cannot begin to develop his musical abilities until he can really listen. Moreover, in developing his auditory discrimination we are tackling one of the key factors involved in the basic literacy skills.

We know that a young child's hearing is usually more acute than that of an adult; we also know, from our experience as classroom teachers, that many children fail to learn because they either won't or can't listen. Is it because they have learnt to close their ears in an effort to survive in a world aurally polluted by blaring transistors, traffic noise and often a noisy home background? Whatever the reason it is clear that one of our first starting points when considering musical activities is to teach the skill of listening, and in order to do this we must understand what is involved.

Firstly the child must *concentrate*: this he will do if he is interested and the length of time for which he will concentrate will depend partly upon his degree of interest.

Secondly he must *understand* what he is listening to: if it is speech, he needs to have developed the necessary vocabulary and concepts that are being used; if it is music or environmental sound, he needs help in the initial recognition and discrimination of the sound and in building up an accurate memory bank (sounds that are near or far away, high or low, human or mechanical, long or short, etc.).

And finally, because of the ephemeral nature of sound, he must learn to *remember* what he has heard: this demands a great deal of practice since discrimination, comparison and sorting are so difficult with sounds – they fade and are gone so quickly!

DEVELOPING LISTENING SKILLS

There are many ways of helping children to listen that can be integrated into the daily programme:

1 Give important instructions that the children should be expected to understand and remember.

2. Ask the children to take messages and to carry out specific duties in the classroom.
3. Invite other adults into the classroom to talk to the children.
4. Listen to and discuss sounds – like a jet liner overhead, an ambulance siren, light or heavy rain, etc.
5. Use the quiet of story time to focus on specific sounds.
6. Use songs and singing games to develop vocabulary and memory (see Chapter 2).

Here are some specific listening games and activities. Adapt them to your own group of children and invent some more of your own.

Sound recognition and discrimination

Body sounds

1. Copy the sound I make (clap, tap, shuffle, snap fingers, any vocal sound). Everyone look.
   Using a screen, back of a bookcase or large carton as a cover, play the same game. Ask a child to make the sound.
2. Three or four children turn their backs or hide behind a screen. One speaks – who is it?
   They all speak except one – who is left out?
3. Whispering chain – a short message is passed round in a circle. How does it become distorted?

Sounds from everyday material

(paper, tin, plastic carton, cup and spoon, sandpaper, pencil, wooden spoon, comb, bunch of keys)

1. Choose two sound makers and listen carefully to the sounds. Hide them (in a box), play quietly and let the children identify them as you play. Next time change the sound makers or add another one.
2. Prepare two sets of about three sound makers (four or more to increase the difficulty). Make a sound. A child watches and then copies.
3. Use a screen or large carton to hide one set and play the same game. Let the children have a go at making the hidden sound.
4. Make two sounds at once (if you can!). Play with both sets visible first and then hide one set.
5. Make pictures of the sound makers you are using. This time when you make a sound the child must select the corresponding picture.
6. Play the last game with the sound makers hidden.
7. Let a volunteer hide (behind a screen, or close eyes and turn away) then put the sound makers into the middle of your

listening circle; one child makes a sound for the hiding child to identify. If he is correct it is his turn to make a sound for the next volunteer to guess.

8 Sound matching – sit the children in a circle and give out three or four different sound makers. A volunteer is given another sound maker that matches one of the four already given out. He is blindfolded, put in the middle of the circle and turned around. The children in the circle now play their sound makers altogether while the player in the middle must find the matching sound to his own and sit in front of that player.

Sounds from instruments

Using percussion instruments instead of sound makers, repeat the activities listed above. With older children or those who have had plenty of practice in sound recognition, try using chimebars. Start with the concept of 'high' and 'low' for the children to identify. If you can, get hold of two sets (e.g. two low 'C's and two high 'C's): play the copying game, hiding one set as suggested in the other activities. If the children can manage this easily, add a 'middle' chimebar (G). Play the sound-matching game using chimebars.

Environmental sounds

1 Near and far: With eyes closed, what can they hear:

(a) in the classroom;
(b) outside but within the building;
(c) outside the school?

With younger children you could discuss the sounds and let the children try to imitate them. With older children try recording the sounds either in writing or drawing.

2 A listening walk: Take the children out one day for a *short* walk and ask them what sounds they can hear. Prepare a sound frieze on your return to accommodate all the sources of the sounds the children heard, and find word sounds to accompany them, for example *zzz, sh, ooo, tch*, etc.

Classify the sounds – loud, quiet, high, low, nice, nasty, near, far away.

3 Now consider 'sets' of sounds – traffic, animal, human, mechanical, musical.

Developing an aural memory

1 Make several different sounds using parts of your body. The children must copy *in the correct sequence*. Hide behind a screen and repeat.

2 Sequence building (for older children): Sit in a circle with the children and start the game by making a sound. Everyone repeats that sound and the next player adds another,

different sound. Everyone copies those two sounds and the next player adds a third (different) sound and so on. See how many sounds you can remember in sequence.

3 Prepare two sets of sound makers (ordinary objects or instruments or a mixture). Sit in a listening circle with one set in the middle. Make a number of sounds on your set and choose a child to copy those sounds *in the correct sequence* on the other set. Extend this by:
   (a) increasing the number of sounds they must copy;
   (b) hiding the set that *you* play.
4 Choose four or more sounds and play all but one – which one was left out?
5 Sing and clap a simple song that the children know well. Clap one part of the song with a distinctive rhythmic pattern, e.g. 'Pitter, patter, raindrops' from 'I hear thunder'. The children must identify the words.
   Cumulative songs also develop the memory through singing (see page 20).
6 Organize a 'listening spree' – either a short spell in the playground, or a short walk. Take a tape recorder. Can the children remember the sequence of sounds they heard? Play back your recording.
7 Try linking a sound signal with movement, e.g. clappers mean run, tambourine – skip, drum – stop, cymbal – sit.
   Begin by using two signals only – run and stop; skip and stop. Now three signals – run, stop, sit; skip, stop, sit. Then mix all four – run, skip, stop, sit; run, stop, skip, sit. . . .

Music corner activities

See Chapter 5.

Using the tape recorder

There are many ways in which the tape recorder can complement and extend these listening games, but unless the recorder is a good one, some distortion of the actual sound is bound to occur on the recording. It is best to delay the use of the recorder for listening until the children have had plenty of experience listening to and focusing upon non-recorded sounds. When they are ready and if your recorder is suitable, try some of these activities:

1 Make a recording of some people (and children) that you all know. Record them one by one at first, then try a recorded conversation with a known group. Can the children recognize their friends and the grown-ups.
2 Record some sounds at home; play them for the children to identify. Some of the children might like to bring in their own sound tapes.

3 Similarly record sounds in the High Street or any local place of interest to the children. Let the children record sounds in school and play them back.
4 Sound lotto – the children each have a card with assorted pictures of the recorded sounds. They cover up each picture when they hear the corresponding sound on their card. Who is the first to finish? (A good commercial kit can be purchased from the Remedial Supply Company, Dixon Street, Wolverhampton WV2 2BX.)
5 Older children can record stories and add their own sound effects.

Using listening games and activities

Begin very simply and build up the children's listening skills gradually and systematically. Here are some guidelines:

1 Encourage the children to listen to sounds on their own, *one at a time.*
2 Then let them compare *two different sounds.*
3 Introduce activities with *two or more different sounds.*
4 Introduce activities with *two or more similar sounds.*
5 Keep all listening games and activities *very quiet* to ensure the maximum concentration.
6 Introduce new activities when the children are *fresh.*

Listening to recorded music

Developing good listening habits through games, singing and activities involving the children's own music making will help them when it comes to listening to recorded music – a whole world of sound that cannot easily be imported live into school. Listening to older brothers or sisters, or children from another school, to musical parents or to a visiting group of musicians will delight young children and should be one of their first and continuing experiences of listening to music; nothing can replace the thrill and impact of an actual performance.

When asking children to listen to recorded music, we often have to take into account the fact that, for many of them, this kind of sound is being fed into their lives all the time through radio, television, cassettes and records, in supermarkets, cafés and other public places as background sound. It is a good idea therefore to relate a specific piece of recorded music to the children's own activities. Use the music in movement sessions and listen again afterwards; link it with a suitable story; use it to stimulate art work when conditions are suitable; introduce a relevant excerpt when the children have been making their own sound pictures – Debussy's 'The Snow is Dancing' from *Children's Corner* Suite when they have been singing and playing about the snow; Haydn's 'Clock' Symphony 101 when they have been practising clocks ticking, and there is some excellent electronic music on the *Listen, Move and Dance* Record No. 4 (HMV/CLP/3531) that would illustrate activities about machines.

Later on the children will be ready to listen more purposefully to recorded music. Keep the listening times *short* (not more than two or three minutes at the most) and ask the children to *listen out for some specific features* of the music they are going to hear, for example: 'Can you hear Peter's tune?' (from *Peter and the Wolf* by Prokofiev); 'When do the clockwork toys stop and then start again?' ('Musique des Automates' from *Coppelia* by Delibes).

It is important that *you* like the music, for the children will quickly catch your enthusiasm, and that the music has a special appeal – perhaps a strong story line, an exciting rhythm or some topical interest. Finally, do let the children *listen often enough* to get to know the music really well; there is a great joy in recognizing something that is already familiar – like meeting an old friend.

Appendix 2 contains a list of suggested records to introduce to young children.

Further reading

There are many excellent musical 'fun' games in *Pompaleerie Jig* by Diana Thompson and Kate Baxter (E.J. Arnold, 1978) and in the practical booklets *Sounds Together* and *Sounds Unlimited* available from ILEA Teachers' Centre for Music, Sutherland Street, London SW1V 4LH. See also the section on 'Musical Games' by Clive Walkley in *Time for Music*, the Schools Council Project for Young Children (E.J. Arnold, 1976), and *Sounds Fun*, a book of musical games for children by Trevor Wishart (Universal Edition, 1977).

2 SINGING IN THE CLASSROOM

Singing together is fun; it is also most children's first experience of group music making and for both children and teacher the importance of regular classroom singing is greater than is often realized. It can stimulate and calm the children, bring class and teacher together and provide an enjoyable, controlled activity to balance the programme of a busy day. It develops the child's musical abilities and social skills while also acting as a valuable aid in reading and language development, in building basic concepts and in linking and extending other areas of the curriculum. It is a good musical starting point and an excellent aid to the teacher, once she is aware of its potential.

ABOUT SINGING

Singing should always be relaxed and enjoyable but this does not mean that we should tolerate sloppy singing or, of course, shouting – which so often happens when the children become excited, overenthusiastic or are told to 'sing up'. Encourage them to sit up comfortably, try to catch the mood of the song and if you all enjoy it the quality of the singing will be right.

The *pitch* at which young children can sing comfortably is lower than is usually thought. However, the range of children's voices increases with age, maturity and experience of daily or frequent correct singing. Given time they will manage (and enjoy) the higher notes. Settle for a comfortable pitch for your own children: this is easily done if you don't worry about accompanying them: classroom singing is usually unaccompanied anyway and this is certainly the best way with young children. One of the tuned instruments will supply a starting note, if needed.

Very few children are tone deaf: some children are merely lazy singers, or don't know the words of the song; others (usually more boys than girls) take longer to learn to pitch their voices than their peers – they are known as 'growlers'! It helps to sit these children next to someone with a strong sense of pitch and to ask them to listen as they sing; they must sing quietly to do this, which is better for them and everyone else anyway. Give them an instrument to play sometimes, so that they are encouraged to keep listening and so that their involvement •

maintains their interest. Never stop them singing. Give them some individual attention. They can be trained!

Developing a sense of pitch

Singing is a valuable activity in helping to develop the child's sense of pitch – that is, the ability to discriminate between high and low sounds, together with an awareness of the relationship of one sound with another and a feeling for a 'home note' or the main sound upon which each tune is based.

A systematic approach to the development of pitch in the child's singing voice can be made through the use of Tonic Sol-fa which employs hand signs and singing names (doh, ray, me, fah, soh, lah, te, doh). This method was used by our own John Curwen, a self-taught musician, and Kodály, the great Hungarian music educator. A full outline does not come within the scope of this book but interested readers are referred to the Appendix, and are recommended to attend a suitable course.

CHOOSING SONGS

There are now many excellent collections of songs available to teachers of young children and the welcome addition of an accompanying cassette makes them much easier to use.

However, choosing a song is still a problem for many of us. What criteria should we adopt? We could choose songs to link with aspects of topic work, with the changing seasons or specific festivals: and the children like to sing about themselves, their homes, lives and interests. Whatever the basis for our choice the following points should also be considered:

1. The song should *appeal to the children*: it may be the tune itself or the rhythm that is attractive; whatever it is if the children like the song and can remember it easily, they will enjoy singing it.
2. The song should *not be too long* and, in general, the younger the child the greater is the need for repetition and for a predictable pattern within each verse.
3. Songs *with a chorus* encourage even shy children to join in.
4. Songs which lend themselves to *movement* often have greater potential with young children.
5. Avoid tunes with *very high notes* or *difficult leaps*.
6. Choose songs with words that the children *understand*. Sometimes it is necessary to explain a particular word; at other times it is better to substitute another word or phrase. Always try out new words to see how they 'sing'.

There are times, however, when the children's response is unpredictable: when, for instance, they sing with ease something you thought might be too difficult; or when, on the other hand, they are markedly unenthusiastic about something you have chosen as very suitable. In the latter case it is best to drop the new song and try again another day, for it may only be the 'newness' that the children didn't like. If, however, it really is the song, then it is best to forget it.

Do not introduce too many new songs in quick succession, for children love to sing something they know. Build on familiar material and keep a file or note of songs that are popular with you and your own group. Aim for a good standard.

Nursery rhymes and repetitive songs

The repetition contained in many nursery rhymes and songs helps the child to build up a store of words and to assimilate much of the structure of language and of the rhythm and use of words. Repetition of words in reading schemes (a necessary element) is often found to be boring, but children actually enjoy repetition in rhymes and songs because it forms an integral part of the overall pattern. They will often read the words of a rhyme or song more readily than lines of prose – the look is less dense on the page and the tune will spur the reader on. Moreover, the habit of good guesses will carry over to prose reading.

Rhymes and songs with repetition provide excellent material for an early approach to 'look and say'. For example:

Polly put the kettle on, — — — — — — — — — — We'll all have tea.	This little pig went to market — — — stayed at home, — — — had roast beef, — — — had none And — — — cried 'Wee-ee-ee I can't find my way home.'

Provide cut-out words for sentence building. They can also provide material for phonic games:

Girls and boys come out to play The moon doth shine as bright as— Leave your supper and leave your sleep And come with your playfellows down the— Come with a whoop, come with a call, Come with a goodwill or not at— Up the ladder and down the— A penny roll will serve us— You find milk and I'll find flour, And we'll have a pudding in half an—	street day all wall hour all

Miss Polly had a dolly who was sick—— She phoned for the doctor to be——— The doctor came with his bag and his hat And he rapped at the door with a———			
sick	quick	rat	sick
quick	tat	quick	tat

Question-and-answer songs

Once the song is well known, divide the class into two groups: one group asks a question, the second group answers. This again underlines patterns in our language as well as giving new interest to a known song.

Here are some examples:

Q: Do you know the Muffin Man?
A: Oh yes I(we) know the Muffin Man.

Q: Polly put the kettle on . . .
A: Suky take it off again . . . (or response)

Q: Mary, Mary, quite contrary . . .
A: With silver bells . . .

Q: Baa, Baa, black sheep, have you any wool?
A: Yes, sir, yes, sir, three bags full . . .

Q: There's a hole in my bucket, dear Liza, dear Liza.
A: Then mend it, dear Georgie . . .[1]

Q: Old woman, old woman, will you come a-shearing?
A: Speak a little louder sir . . .[1]

There are other ways of dividing into groups:

Girls: She sat 'neath the lilacs and played her guitar,
Boys: He sat down beside her and smoked his cigar.[2]

In a cottage in a wood . . .
Group 1: 'Help me, help me, help me,' he said
'Or the hunter will shoot me dead.'
Group 2: 'Come little rabbit, stay with me,
Happy you will be!'[2]

Large group: There were ten in the bed
And the little one said,
Small group: 'Roll over! Roll over!'
Large group: So they all rolled over and one fell out . . .[1]

Making up words

The rhythm and tune of many songs and rhymes provide a good framework for children to begin making up their own songs or parts of them. Trying to fit words into a tune will alert children to the *rhythm* of words and the extent to which they can successfully do this will depend upon their vocabulary and language development. It is important that you encourage them however clumsy their early attempts may be and if you introduce this activity frequently enough, skill with words will gradually build up.

Start very simply, changing just one or two words:

Do you know the Muffin Man (bus driver, milkman, etc.)
Who lives in Drury Lane? (East Finchley, Manchester, etc.)

Here we go round the mulberry bush (classroom, playground, apple tree, etc.)

Miss Polly had a dolly . . .[1] (teddy, pussy, etc.)

Take you riding in my car, car . . .[5] (van, bus, taxi, lorry, etc.)

The bear went over the mountain . . .[1] (donkey, horse, my friend, etc.)

Progress to longer phrases or complete lines:

(to the tune of 'Polly put the kettle on')
Polly lay the table (3 times)
We'll all have tea.

Suky do the washing up (3 times)
They've all gone away.

What other things can Polly and Suky do at teatime? The children can also substitute their own names and activities.

What shall we do when we all go out, all go out, all go out,
What shall we do when we all go out, all go out to play?[5]

Children answer:

We will climb on the climbing frame . . .
We will swim in the swimming pool . . .
We will rock on the rocking horse . . .[3]

Leaving off the last word

This is a very popular game with the added advantage of training the memory and a feeling for pulse. Sing the song right through. The second time leave off the last word. Then leave off the last two words and so on. Choose a song with repeat lines:

Heads, shoulders, knees and toes[2]

John Brown's baby's got a cold upon his chest[2]

Johnny taps with one hammer[2] (keep to one verse)

One finger, one thumb, keep moving[2] (keep to one verse)

The bear went over the mountain[1]

She'll be coming round the mountain[1]

Adapting songs Sometimes it is difficult to find just the right song; this can provide a strong incentive to 'do it yourself'. Certain songs lend themselves to adaptation and children are often very quick at spotting this. Consider these variations:

The wheels on the bus go round and round . . .[4]
The streamers in the wind go to and fro . . .
The bubbles in the air go up and down . . .
My little baby doll goes fast asleep . . .

Daddy's taking us to the zoo tomorrow . . .[1]
Mummy's taking us to the shops tomorrow . . .
Granny's taking us to the park tomorrow . . .
David's taking me on the tube tomorrow . . .

Down at the station early in the morning . . .[4]
Down at the seaside sitting in the water . . .
Down with the farmer feeding all the chickens . . .
Down in the playground early in the morning . . .

Cumulative songs The songs that add an extra bit to each verse are an excellent aid in training the children's auditory memory. The children enjoy the challenge and the momentum of the song will cause them to *think ahead*. Get them to draw *pictures*: mount these and print the *words* on the back. These can be used as prompters, the pictures first, later the words according to your group, until the sequence is memorized. They could also provide the basis for a frieze or class picture/reading book. Start with two or three verses with young children and only attempt the other verses if you think the children can manage them and still enjoy the song.

Old MacDonald had a farm[5] (adds animals)

I jump out of bed in the morning[2] (adds actions)

One finger, one thumb, keep moving[2] (adds parts of the body)

All in the wood there grew a tree[5] (adds branch, nest, bird, wing, feather)

Bought me a cat, the cat pleased me[3] (adds hen, duck, goose, dog, sheep, cow, horse)

There was an old woman who swallowed a fly[1] (adds spider, bird, cat, dog, goat, cow, horse)

When I first came to this land[6] (adds duck, cow, wife, donkey, son)

Counting songs

Forwards

The Grocers

Our grocer worked hard weighing rice,
Two grocers worked hard packing spice,
Three grocers worked hard sorting teas,
Four grocers worked hard wrapping cheese,
Five grocers worked hard stacking jam,
Six grocers worked hard slicing ham,
Seven grocers worked hard cutting meats,
Eight grocers worked hard opening sweets,
Nine grocers worked hard selling bread,
Ten grocers, tired out, went home to bed.
Barbara Ireson

The elephants (see page 31)
One man went to mow[4]
Peter works with one hammer[4]
Number one, number one, now my song has just begun (page 26)
John Brown had a little Indian (see page 27)
One little brown bird, up and up he flew (see page 28)

Backwards

Seven little dwarfs (see page 30)
Ten green bottles hanging on the wall (traditional)
Five little ducks went swimming one day[4]
Five currant buns in the baker's shop[4]
Ten miles from home (see page 29)
Ten fat sausages sitting in the pan[4]
Five little field mice fast asleep (see page 28)
Five little speckled frogs[7]

There are many ways of using these songs to help with the building of mathematical concepts. They can be turned into action songs, singing games, used with counters, toys or puppets and number flashcards.

Rounds

Certain songs lend themselves to this simple form of part singing, when one half of the class starts singing *after* the first half has already begun.

Singing in rounds develops the children's powers of concentration, but it will depend upon their previous singing experience, their maturity, and your enthusiasm as to whether they are ready for round singing.

Here are a few golden rules that will help your first attempts:

1 The tune itself must be *simple* and *easily learnt.*
2 The children must *know the tune*, so it is better to delay the round until the second, third or fourth time of singing.
3 Sing *quietly* so that both parts can hear one another.
4 *Maintain a strict tempo* in both groups, otherwise the whole things goes to pieces. It is often a good idea to enlist the help of another adult to ensure success at the beginning. Do not leave your children with a sense of frustration or failure.
5 Introduce variety by:
   (a) singing the round several times through – quietly, loudly, quietly again.
   (b) stopping both parts simultaneously, instead of leaving the second group to finish on their own. The parts will then stop on different notes.

Some rounds to begin with:

London's burning
I hear thunder (or Frère Jacques)
Row, row, row your boat
Down in the forest (see page 32)

TEACHING A NEW SONG

Learn the song first so that you can sing it without the book; get another teacher or a musical friend to help you, or use an accompanying tape if there is one. This way you can often tell beforehand if the song is right for your group, whether the words are suitable and 'sing' well. The children themselves will finally confirm your choice but it is important that you give the song a fair trial by being well acquainted with it beforehand.

Don't worry if you feel that your voice isn't good enough. It is more important at this stage to emphasize the enjoyment of singing together and to build up the confidence of all the children, especially the shy ones. They will respond far more positively to a voice that they know than to a tape recorder or to an accompanying instrument, and their singing skills will only develop once they have begun to enjoy using their voices. Our first concern is to encourage all children to enjoy singing, by providing opportunities for them to sing and joining in ourselves.

Sit with the children and briefly introduce the song: 'Here's a song about cuckoos: do you remember we learnt about the way they lay their eggs in other birds' nests . . .?' Then sing the song right through so that the children can absorb the tune and words (page 32). *Sing directly to the children*, looking at them as you do in storytime; you are after all telling them a story through the song.

There is often a part of the song that is repetitive – a chorus, or in the case of this song, the 'cuckoos'. This is the first part the children can join in when you sing the song through again. With a short, simple song you can probably go on to introduce the rest of it immediately; otherwise sing it through once or twice, getting the children to join in on the easy lines and complete the teaching the next time.

Examples of similar songs with joining-in phrases:

Apusski-dusky (joining in 'Apusski dusky, Apusskidu.')[1]

Indians (joining in 'Tom, tom, tom, Too, too, too.')[7]

Train is a-coming (joining in 'Oh yes!')[1]

My ship sailed from China (joining in 'Like this, like this, like this.')[1]

Songs for younger children should be simple, repetitive and short. They can be taught by linking them with movement (as with finger plays):

A witch wears a long tall hat, (arms above head)
A witch has a big black cat. (mime cat)
She sits on a broomstick as she goes by, (stretch arm out)
And 'Oo-oo-oo-oo-oo-ooh' is her cry.[5]

Songs that are built on a *repetitive word pattern* like 'Rabbit ain't got'[1] almost teach themselvs once the tune is absorbed. The only tricky bit in the case of this song is the last line in every verse (there are six):

Rabbit ain't got no tail at all
Tail at all, tail at all,
Rabbit ain't got no tail at all
Just a powder puff.

A visual cue is a good teaching aid to get the song well established. Don't teach too many verses at once, but build up gradually.

Songs that do not use this kind of framework (like 'Apusskidu', which is more in the nature of a narrative) need attention to each verse. The easiest and quickest way – once you have introduced the song as already suggested – is to get the children to echo you, line by line. Link the lines together and then try the whole verse. Do not try to teach more than one verse at a time, but sing the other verses through for continuity, with the children joining in on the repeat words.

Take the boredom out of repetition by asking groups of children to sing in turn through the song – the children over here, those at the back, all those wearing a pullover, etc. Change the speed of the singing; sing very quietly, or a little louder.

Rhythmic difficulties can often be sorted out by clapping through the song. If the tune isn't quite right get the children to sing it to 'la', or hum it. Humming will also help correct raucous singing.

SINGING GAMES

Singing games can be enjoyed by children of all ages. They do not need an instrumental accompaniment, so they can take place virtually anywhere – in the playground, hall or even the classroom. Most classrooms are adaptable: a few desks can be moved, chairs can be stacked and if necessary children can take turns, some playing the game, some watching. They can *all* sing!

There is something especially attractive to children in traditional ring games, many of which keep alive fragments of our past history and bygone customs and ceremonies. Their educational value lies not only in this association and in the enjoyment they bring to children, but also in the contribution they make to the development of self-discipline, social cooperation and the senses of rhythm and pitch. Body movements and actions go naturally with the music and the simplicity of the tunes is suitable for young children's immature voices.

Listed below are some singing games for the classroom, roughly graded, beginning with those more suitable for younger children. There are many more to be found in the sources given in the Bibliography as well as those brought into this country by children from overseas. Get the children or their parents to sing them to you and help you teach them.

Ring O' Roses[8]
Mulberry Bush[5 and 8]
Sally go-round-the Moon[6]
The big ship sails on the Alley-Alley O[6 and 8]
The farmer's in his den[5 and 8]
Poor Jenny is a-weeping[8]
London Bridge is falling down[6 and 8]

The Bridge at Avignon[8]
When I was a young girl[9] or
Did you ever see a lassie[2]
We all clap hands together[8]
Briar Rosebud[5 and 9]
Round and round the village[6 and 8]
Lubin (or Looby) Loo[2 and 8]
Down by the river (see page 33)
Floating down the river (see page 34)
Bow bow bow Belinda (see page 35)
Going to Boston (see page 36)

Further reading

There are a number of suitably **adaptable songs** in the books *Sing-a-Song One* and *Sing-a-Song Two* by Wendy Bird and Gary McAuliffe (Nelson, 1978) with suggestions to start you off.

Further ideas for **rounds** will be found in *Sing a Round* by Mabel Wilson (Oxford University Press, 1964); *Graded Rounds for Recorders/Voices* (Books 1 and 2) by Anne Mendoza (Novello, 1963); *A First Round Book* by Kenneth Simpson (Novello, 1959) and 77 *Rounds and Canons* by Kenneth Simpson (Novello, 1980).

Number one

Traditional
Words by Jean Gilbert

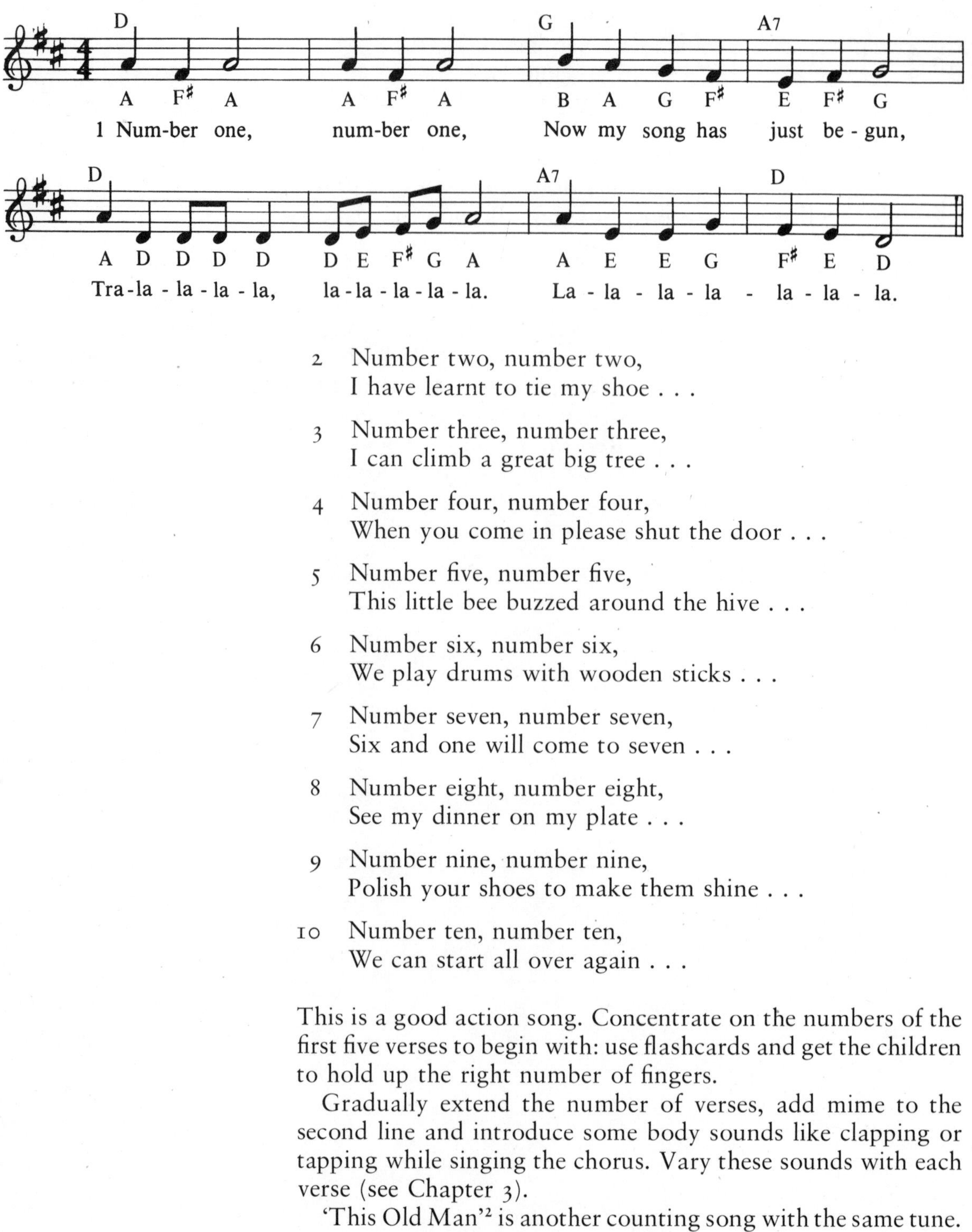

2 Number two, number two,
I have learnt to tie my shoe . . .

3 Number three, number three,
I can climb a great big tree . . .

4 Number four, number four,
When you come in please shut the door . . .

5 Number five, number five,
This little bee buzzed around the hive . . .

6 Number six, number six,
We play drums with wooden sticks . . .

7 Number seven, number seven,
Six and one will come to seven . . .

8 Number eight, number eight,
See my dinner on my plate . . .

9 Number nine, number nine,
Polish your shoes to make them shine . . .

10 Number ten, number ten,
We can start all over again . . .

This is a good action song. Concentrate on the numbers of the first five verses to begin with: use flashcards and get the children to hold up the right number of fingers.

Gradually extend the number of verses, add mime to the second line and introduce some body sounds like clapping or tapping while singing the chorus. Vary these sounds with each verse (see Chapter 3).

'This Old Man'[2] is another counting song with the same tune. It is a good version for older children.

John Brown had a little Indian from *This Little Puffin*

Guitar chords are easier in D. Capo up 3 frets and use chords D, A, A_7.

This counting game can be played on the fingers or as a singing game with children in the middle. It can be readily adapted to 'John Brown had a little motor car' (bicycle, red bus, taxi, etc.) and the names of one of the children used. Finish each verse with a 'Beep, beep' or 'Beep-beep, beep-beep' for his car, etc. – try getting a toy motor horn! Use decorated paper plates as driving wheels and let the children put hats on to indicate what kind of drivers they are.

See if the children can sing the chorus backwards!

One little brown bird

Traditional

C F G7 C

E F F G C C′ C′ B A G E

1 One lit - tle brown bird, up and up he flew, A -

C F G7 C

E F F G G A A E D C

long came a - noth - er one and that made two.

2 Two little brown birds sitting on a tree,
Along came another one and that made three.

3 Three little brown birds hopping on the floor,
Along came another one and that made four.

4 Four little brown birds flying round a hive . . .

5 Five little brown birds pecking at some sticks . . .

6 Six little brown birds flying up to heaven . . .

7 Seven little brown birds sitting on a gate . . .

8 Eight little brown birds perched upon a line . . .

9 Nine little brown birds went to mother hen,
Along came another one and that made ten.

Five little field mice

by Cynthia Raza

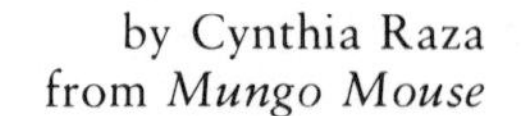

2 Four little field mice . . .

3 Three little field mice . . .

4 Two little field mice . . .

5 One little field mouse . . .

6 No little field mice . . .

Guitar can play in a lower key for younger children. Use chords E, A, B_7.

Percussion Encourage all the children to clap, or make a suitable body sound, on the word 'scoot!' Later introduce an instrument (a drum or a tambourine) for one or two children to play.

This song can underline the concepts of *loud* (owl's hoot) and *quiet* (mice fast asleep). Sing the last verse very, very quietly!

Ten miles from home

Traditional
from *Singing Fun*

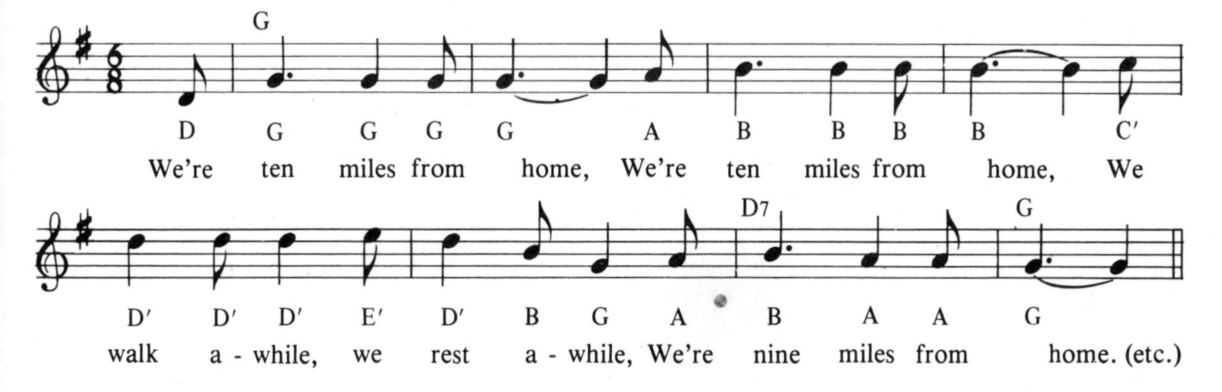

2 We're nine miles from home,
We're nine miles from home,
We walk awhile, we rest awhile,
We're eight miles from home . . .

Last verse ends 'And now we are home.'

Guitar can play in a lower key for younger children. Use chords D, A_7.

This song could be linked with a story, the teacher and the children improvising an account of what could happen at each stop. The concepts of *fast* and *slow* could also be introduced by deciding at what speed each part of the journey is made.

Seven little dwarfs

Melody and words by Jean Gilbert

2 Six little dwarfs went to work one day,
Over the hills and far away.
One little dwarf got stung by a bee,
And five little dwarfs came home to tea.

3 Five little dwarfs went to work one day,
Over the hills and far away.
One little dwarf got stuck in a tree,
And four little dwarfs came home to tea.

4 Four little dwarfs went to work one day,
Over the hills and far away.
One little dwarf ran off to the sea,
And three little dwarfs came home to tea.

5 Three little dwarfs went to work one day,
Over the hills and far away.
One little dwarf fell and hurt his knee,
And two little dwarfs came home to tea.

6 Two little dwarfs went to work one day,
Over the hills and far away.
One little dwarf lost his front door key,
And one little dwarf came home to tea.

7 One little dwarf went to work one day,
Over the hills and far away.
Snow White helped him to find his friends,
And they all came home to tea.

The elephants

from *More Songs for Music Time*

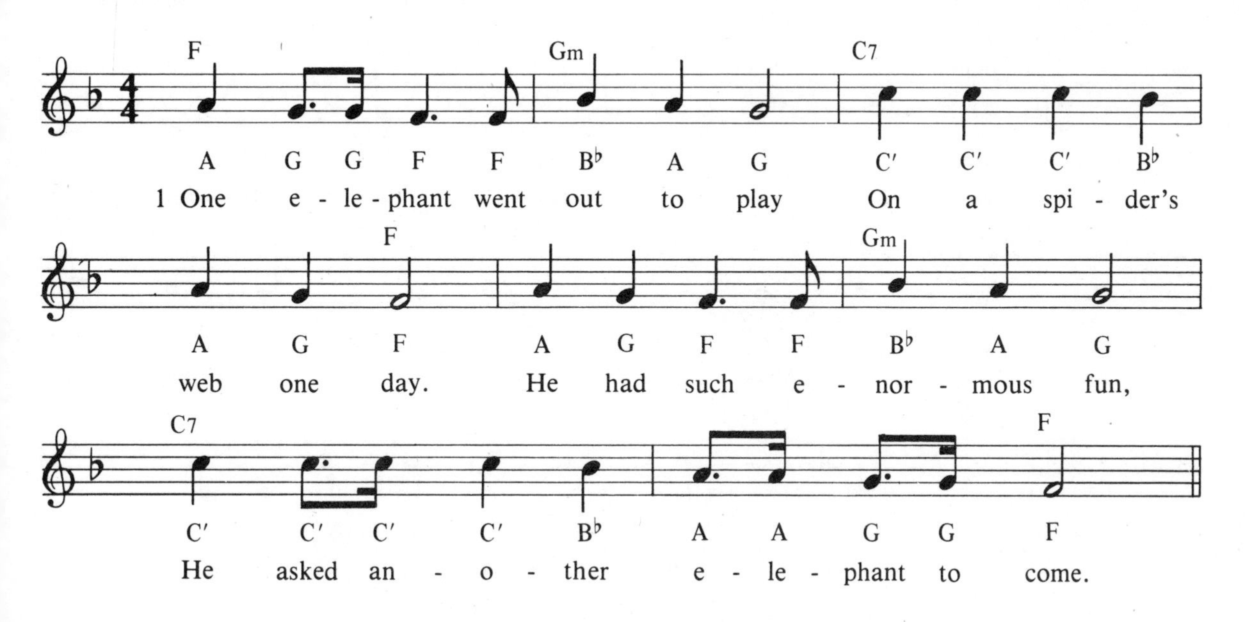

2 Two elephants went out to play
On a spider's web one day.
They had such enormous fun,
They asked another elephant to come.

Guitar chords are easier in D. Capo up 3 frets and use chords D, Em, A_7.

Start with one drum for one elephant and add an extra percussion instrument to each verse as the song proceeds. Let the children play their own accompaniment. Perhaps one child can improvise on a glockenspiel, xylophone, shaker, etc. to suggest the spider's web in bars 3 and 4.

The children can invent their own words:

One kangaroo . . . jumping up and down all day.
One little puppy . . . up and down the path one day.

Singing game Sing the song in a circle with the 'animals' in the middle and the children playing instruments on the outside. Change direction each time another player is chosen.

Down in the forest

French (adapted by Anne Mendoza)
from *Graded Rounds for Recorders or Voices Book 1*

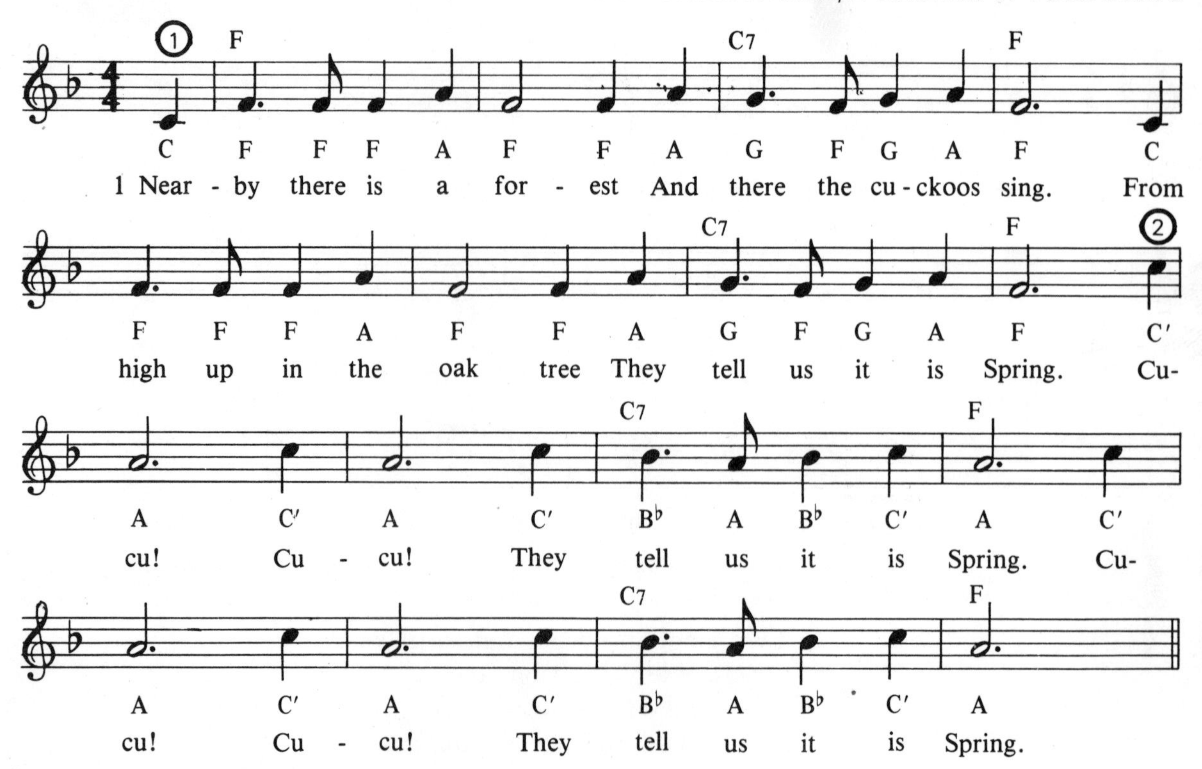

2 Far off in yonder forest
An owl is out of sight
From high up in the oak tree
He tells us it is night.
Hoo-oo! Hoo-oo! } repeat
He tells us it is night. }

Guitar chords are easier in D. Capo in 3 frets and use chords D, A_7.

Optional chimes C′ and A on all the 'cu-cu's and 'hoo-oo's.

Round The song can be sung as a round, the second group starting when the first group reaches ②.

Adapting the song Think of some more verses about other birds in the locality:

Nearby we have a green park and there the ducks can swim . . .
Nearby there is a reservoir and there the geese fly high . . .

Down by the river

London singing game

Verse
Susan, Susan, won't you come to tea?
Come next Saturday at half past three,
Tea-cakes, pancakes and everything you see,
Oh, won't we have a lovely time at half past three.

Singing game Younger children can sing this sitting in a circle while one child 'mimes' in the centre.

Older children will enjoy walking round in a circle, singing, while one child 'washes clothes' in the centre. Change the name 'Mary' in the chorus. The verse is sung by the centre player, who 'calls' a friend, 'Simon, Simon, won't you come to tea?'. Simon sits in the centre, changing places with the caller and the game continues with a new child singing the verse each time.

Floating down the river (Jump Josie) from *Jim along, Josie*

Guitar chords are easier in D. Capo up 3 frets and use chords D, G, A_7.

Singing game Children join hands and circle slowly while one child in the middle chooses a partner. Then at 'Two in the middle' everyone stands still, sings and claps while the two in the middle dance or jump up and down. Continue with four and eight; then finish with 'Get out of here if you can't jump Josie'. The children in the middle slip out and the song starts again. A lovely singing game to underline contrasting speeds.

Bow, bow, bow, Belinda

from Virginia, USA

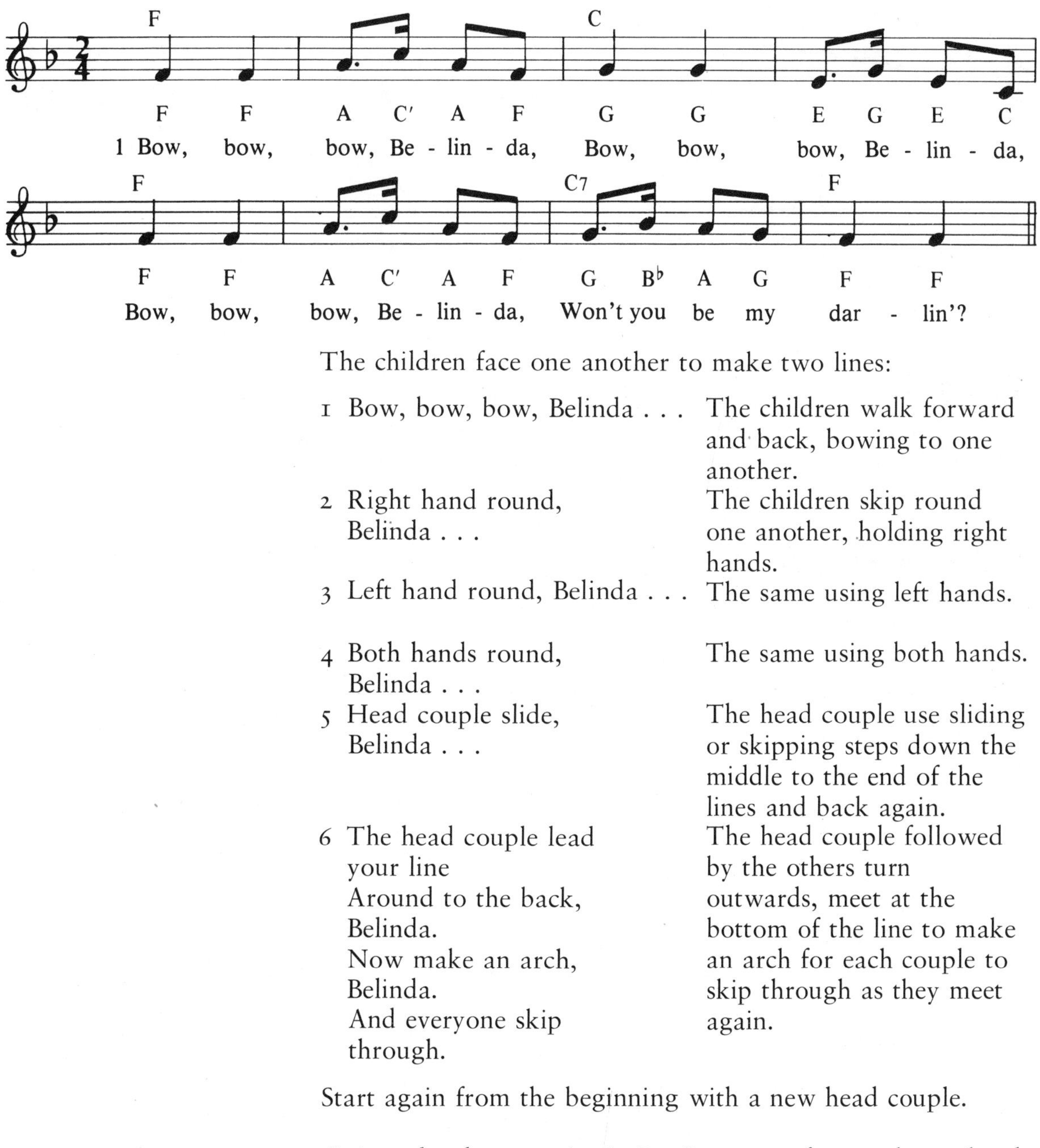

The children face one another to make two lines:

1 Bow, bow, bow, Belinda . . .	The children walk forward and back, bowing to one another.
2 Right hand round, Belinda . . .	The children skip round one another, holding right hands.
3 Left hand round, Belinda . . .	The same using left hands.
4 Both hands round, Belinda . . .	The same using both hands.
5 Head couple slide, Belinda . . .	The head couple use sliding or skipping steps down the middle to the end of the lines and back again.
6 The head couple lead your line Around to the back, Belinda. Now make an arch, Belinda. And everyone skip through.	The head couple followed by the others turn outwards, meet at the bottom of the line to make an arch for each couple to skip through as they meet again.

Start again from the beginning with a new head couple.

Guitar chords are easier in D. Capo up 3 frets and use chords D, A, A_7.

This is an enjoyable singing game for older children. To begin with, use the first four verses only so that the children can enjoy the movements thus far. For the last two verses the columns shouldn't be too long.

Going to Boston

A Kentucky song
from *Jim along, Josie*

2 Saddle up, boys, and let's go with them.
Saddle up, boys, and let's go with them.
Saddle up, boys, and let's go with them,
Early in the morning.
Chorus

3 Swing your partner all the way to Boston,
Swing your partner all the way to Boston,
Swing your partner all the way to Boston,
Early in the morning.
Chorus

Singing game A line of boys faces a line of girls:

1 Following the leader, the line of girls skips around the boys, coming back in time for the chorus, which all clap and sing in place for each verse.
2 The line of boys gallops around the girls and back to place for the chorus.
3 The girls and boys opposite each other take hands and skip gently in a two-handed swing, again lining up in time to sing and clap the chorus.

3 PERCUSSION

Most children have a natural sense of rhythm. Even before birth the foetus is experiencing the rhythmic heartbeat of its mother and the warmth and known rhythm of the mother nursing her new-born baby bring security and contentment. She will sing to the baby and rock him gently if he is fretful. She will dance the baby on her lap, sing 'Pat-a-cake, pat-a-cake, baker's man' when he is playful. The baby is experiencing rhythm in many ways, and if lucky will continue to enjoy action songs and rhythm games in the family, with friends and perhaps in a nursery or playgroup. Unfortunately, there are children who, through a number of reasons – family break up, an overworked working mother – miss out on these early experiences. They will need all the opportunities we can give them in the nursery and reception class, to sing, dance, play and move to music, for *it is this experience of using the whole body in rhythmic movement that will in turn lead to a confident use of percussion instruments later on.*

At first, very young children should be encouraged to move freely to discover their own rhythms and to develop the necessary degree of body control that will enable them to respond later to the more specific rhythms of walking, marching, running, skipping, galloping and to the different ways of moving – fast, slow, light, bouncy, heavy, etc. All this helps when it comes to the finer body movements we use in our finger plays and speech rhymes.

INTRODUCING BODY SOUNDS AND MOVEMENTS

The child's first natural percussion instrument is his own body, especially his hands; if we give him plenty of opportunity to make his own 'body' sounds as he joins in with rhythm games, songs and rhymes, he will be much more at home with instruments later on. Apart from being easier to do, these movements – clapping, tapping feet, clicking fingers, slapping thighs, making vocal sounds – enable him to feel the rhythm as a physical experience. Nothing can replace this early stage and it should remain an important ingredient of rhythmic activities with all infant and junior children.

We can begin very simply:

Peter works with one hammer, One hammer, one hammer, Peter works with one hammer, All day long.[4]	*Children keep the rhythm by tapping one hand on one knee.*

Five currant buns in the baker's shop,	*Hold up five fingers.*
Big and round with sugar on the top,	*Make a big circle with arms and tap rhythmically on the head.*
Along came a boy (Johnny) with a penny one day,	*Johnny gets up to buy a bun.*
Bought a currant bun and took one away.	*All hold out a 'penny' and clap on 'took one away'.*

I can knock with my two hands,	*Knock, knock, knock.*
I can rock with my two hands,	*Rock, rock, rock.*
I can tap with my two hands,	*Tap, tap, tap.*
I can clap with my two hands.[10]	*Clap, clap, clap.*

The children can think of more things to do.

Wind the bobbin up, wind the bobbin up,	*Roll hands round each other.*
Pull, pull, clap, clap, clap;	*Pull fists apart and clap.*
Point to the ceiling, point to the floor, Point to the window, point to the door, Clap your hands together, one, two, three, Put your hands upon your knee.[4]	*Do all the actions rhythmically.*

We all clap hands together, We all clap hands together, We all clap hands together, And have a jolly time.[8]	*Quiet rhythmic clapping throughout.*

Clap or tap on the chorus of songs like 'Going to the zoo' and 'This old man'.

Clapping games

Aim to do as much rhythmic clapping as possible, then clapping games can be fun and more spontaneous.

1 Sing and clap with the children a well-known song like 'I

hear thunder', then clap a phrase from the song that has a marked rhythm pattern like 'patter, patter, rain drops', and ask the children which bit was clapped.

2 Display pictures of two songs or nursery rhymes that the children know, and sing and clap them through with the children. Clap one of them; the children must guess which one. Try three pictures when you think the children are ready.

3 Echo clapping: See if the children can copy what you have clapped. It is fun beginning with word association, for all children seem to be fascinated by the rhythms of words. They will enjoy it if you begin with their own names! Clap and whisper the words, keeping to their natural rhythms (● = 1 clap):

Susan Virginia Anthony Wayne

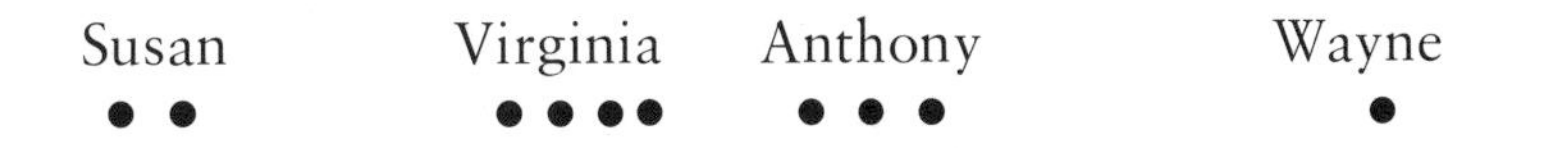

The children clap and whisper as an echo. Then try longer phrases.

Hallo children Please shut the door Sausages and mash

See if one of the children can think of something to clap for *you* to echo.

4 Which one did I clap? Display two children's name cards and clap one. The child with that name must clap back. Extend by using three and perhaps four name cards. Try a similar game using prepared cards illustrating the short phrases you have used.

Rhythm games This game is a good 'gatherer' and is particularly suitable for the playground. Clap a pattern and keep repeating it until all the children have got it; then change the pattern and keep clapping until all have mastered the change. Keep it very rhythmic:

Repeat.

Change to:

Repeat.

Change to:

Repeat.

Notice that only one change is made at a time.

> = Emphasize the first beat.

= one clap (crotchet)

= two quick claps (quavers)

The next stage, a classroom activity, is to teach a simple rhythm by clapping and then ask the children to transfer the same rhythm to knees, shoulders, feet, etc. This should be played continuously by the children and changes made only when they are all responding rhythmically on the correct part of the body. One child could lead the others.

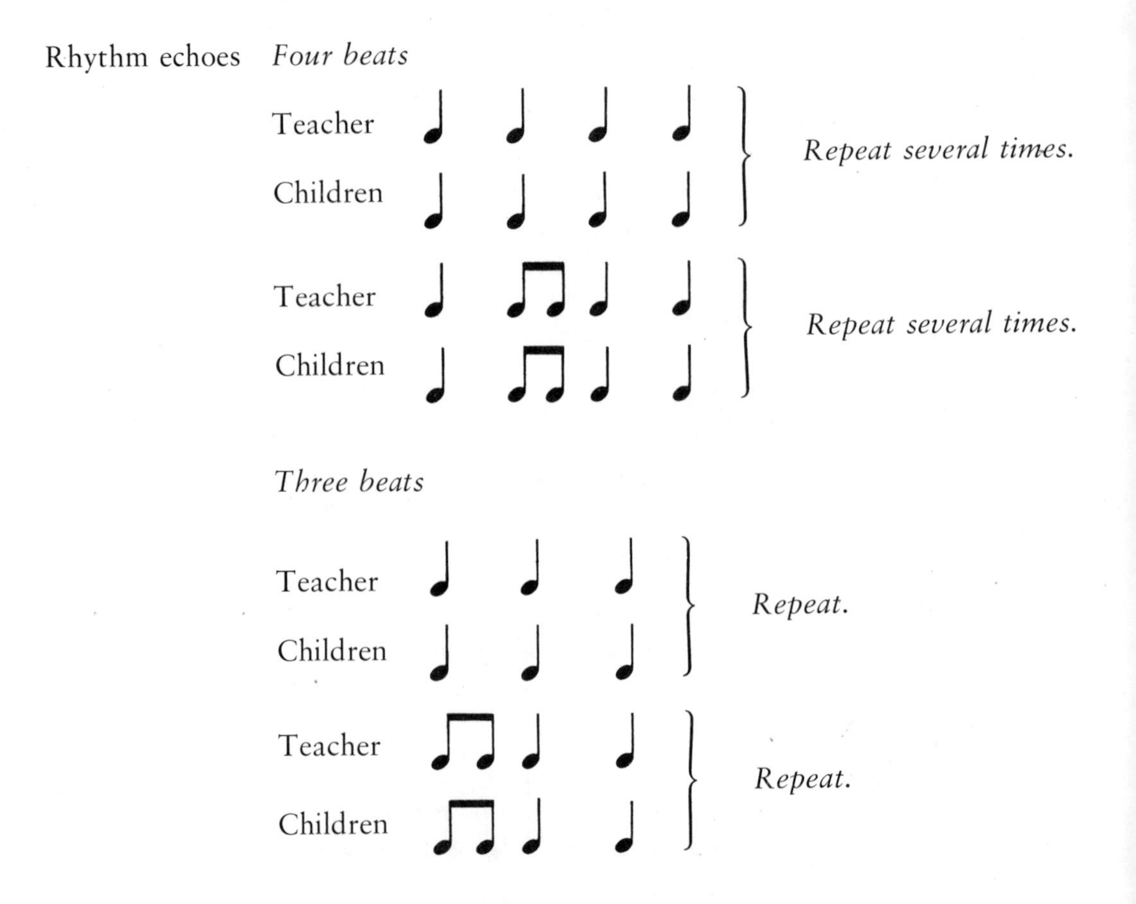

In order to get an *immediate* echo, it is important to keep a strict rhythm. One child could keep a drumbeat going and the teacher could mime listening for the echo.

Songs and rhythm games for older children

Here are examples of *joining-in songs* suitable for use with older children. The children can make their own body sounds and later on use instruments where suitable.

If you're happy and you know it clap your hands (clap, clap)[1]
Let everyone clap hands like me (clap, clap)[2]
Everybody do this[2]
Clap, clap, clap your hands[3]
Who's that tapping at the window[3]
Land of the Silver Birch[6]
Three sailors went to sea[6]
Clapping Land[6]
Bingo[6]

Chorus songs: Down in Demerara[1]
She sat 'neath the lilacs[2]
One potato, two potato[1]

You can now begin to mix the movements:

Here	we	sit	like	birds in the wilderness
clap	*click*	*clap*	*click*	etc. (from 'Down in Demerara')

Um	chinga-a	chinga,	um	chinga-chinga		
slap knees	*clap*	*clap*	*knees*	*clap*	*clap*	etc.

(from 'She sat 'neath the lilacs')

Older children who have had plenty of exercise in simple body sounds will enjoy these rhythm games:

Divide into two groups. Appoint leaders who decide on a rhythm and way of playing, for example:

Group 1 ♩ ♩ ♩ ♩ *clapping*

Group 2 ♩ ♫ ♩ ♩ *slapping knees*

Progress to:

(a) the use of more difficult rhythms, possibly using the rhythms of words to help;
(b) each group using two movements;

(c) dividing into three or four groups;
(d) stopping and restarting groups from time to time.

Always keep the same number of beats and a continuous beat on a drum or tambour to keep everyone together.

Once the children have mastered these activities, the games can be played using instruments:

Using three beats and two groups

Using word rhythms

I have suggested beginning with names and short phrases using the natural rhythm of the spoken language. This can be extended with older children and linked with words related to ongoing topics or centres of interest. Boost the reading by preparing simple cards:

car	lorry	bicycle	van
●	● ●	● ● ●	●

submarine	tanker	liner	ship
● ● ●	● ●	● ●	●

glider	jumbo jet	D C 10	Trident
● ●	● ● ●	● ● ●	● ●

1 Start as before with two word rhythms on one card and extend according to the children's ability. Practise each card this way:

(a) Read the card several times, concentrating on the rhythm.
(b) *Say* and *clap* rhythmically several times.
(c) *Whisper* and *clap* rhythmically several times.
(d) *Think* the words and *clap* rhythmically.

(This idea was originally outlined in *Topic Anthologies* by Jean Gilbert (Oxford University Press) and is illustrated by workcards for the music corner.)

2 Play the game 'Which one did I clap?'. Let the children have a go. Whoever guesses correctly can then choose another card to clap. And so on. Leave the cards in the music corner for the children to continue the game with a friend. Put out one or two simple instruments like rhythm sticks, so that the children can now try playing the rhythms.

3 Choose two cards: Divide into two groups, give each group one card to clap and let them clap at the same time one set of rhythms against the other.

4 Choose one card: Clap and say it three times, gradually getting louder.
Clap and say it three times, gradually getting quieter.
Clap and say it three times, getting gradually louder then quieter.

5 Divide into two groups: Clap and whisper three times as a round, getting louder and quieter as practised above, for example:

Group 1: car lorry bicycle van car lorry bicycle
● ● ● ● ● ● ● ● ● ● ● ● ●

Group 2: car lorry bicycle van car
● ● ● ● ● ● ● ●

6 Investigate different categories of words like food, car, flowers, streets.
7 Older children will enjoy using names of football clubs, pop groups, favourite TV programmes.

There are many activities stemming from these variations on a theme; one of them is to use these rhythms as a basis for tune making (described in Chapter 4).

INTRODUCING PERCUSSION SOUND

One of the best ways of introducing very young children to the use of percussion sound is to use it yourself in storytime and with your finger plays and action songs.

Stories

Many stories lend themselves to sound effects; a first telling is usually a special occasion but it is often on the second and third time round that the children will want to join in. They will learn a lot about the handling of their sound makers through their contribution in storytime.

The Three Billy Goats Gruff
You could use clappers played in three different ways to represent the Billy Goats Gruff going over the bridge, a rubber drum to represent the roaring troll and some noisy bells for the troll's final splash down!

The Three Bears
Try three different-toned rubber drums, bongos or tambours to accompany the different voices of the three bears and to underline the rhythm of 'Who's been eating *my* porridge?' etc.

The Emperor's Nightingale
Try to get a bird whistle or use a group of good whistlers from your class. The clockwork bird is wound up with a golden key – use a guiro or corregated card. How would you contrast the real bird with the clockwork toy? . . . There's a clock chiming – triangle or chimebar – and bell sounds in the Emperor's garden.

Try making up your own stories with special sound effects – domestic sounds; different kinds of bells and clocks; traffic sounds; animal sounds. Have your own collection of sound effects near at hand for storytime.

It is a good idea to follow up interest aroused by a good 'sound' story by leaving the instruments you have used in the music corner with a suitable picture (see Chapter 5 for further ideas for the music corner).

Finger plays and action songs

Percussion sounds can add new interest to many old favourites:

(a) To underline the story narrative:

Incy Wincy Spider climbed up the water spout (shakers)
Down came the rain and washed poor Incy out (tambourine or bells)
Out came the sunshine and dried up all the rain (a few chimes)
And Incy Wincy Spider climbed that spout again.[1] (shakers)

(b) To underline actions, creatures, etc:

Ten fat sausages sizzling in the pan,
One went pop (clapper) and the other went bang! (drum)[1]

Swish, little fish, in water clear (shaker)
Fly, little bird, up in the air; (bells)
Creep, little caterpillars, creep, (sand-block)
Sleep, little children, softly sleep.[1]

In the music corner

Children can handle instruments and sound makers in their own time – following up a 'sound' story or song, or investigating specific aspects of sound (see Chapter 4).

TRAINING IN THE USE OF INSTRUMENTS

With young children it is best to use home-made instruments (see Chapter 6) and to organize specific sessions when all the children can use them together – up to 20 or 25 is feasible, but as a general rule the younger the child, the smaller the group needs to be. A good time to start is when the children have been in school for about half a term and have been introduced to percussion sound as already suggested. It is a good idea to store the instruments in the classroom or within easy reach and to start with *morning* sessions when the children are fresh. Use instruments that the children have already been handling; limit the variety and the number of 'loud' ones like clappers.

For a group of twenty, the following is sufficient:

(5) a small selection of datebox clappers or rhythm sticks;
(10) a larger selection of shakers;
(5) a selection of rubber drums or similar sound makers; (plus extras to avoid squabbling).

Sit in a circle (in a carpeted area if possible) round the instruments, let each child choose one quickly and keep it quiet until everyone is ready. Accustom the children to this training – it will make group percussion sessions so much more enjoyable – but make *as quick a start as you can*! Use hand signals (see illustrations) to conduct the children, explaining at first what is meant by each signal.

Repeat until the children are used to watching you *all the time*.

Repeat several times and then alternate loud playing with very quiet, controlled playing. Ask one group of instruments (and possibly individual children) to play on their own. Always use the same hand signals.

Now choose two contrasted well-known songs – 'The Grand Old Duke of York' and 'Bye, Baby Bunting', for instance – and let the children sing and play, having decided *how* to play each time.

The next time introduce quick and slow:

Introduce variety by getting the children to:

1 play quickly then slowly, loudly then quietly, in groups and on their own;
2 choose a well-known song; sing and play it quickly, then slowly;
3 sing and play two suitable songs, one loudly, the other very quietly.

In later sessions progress to:

getting louder

getting quieter

getting louder
then quieter

similarly with faster and slower. Invent your own conducting signs.

Then try:
loudly *and* quickly or slowly
quietly *and* quickly or slowly.

These graduated movements demand great control. Don't introduce them too soon, or too many at a time!

Now invent a conducting sign for *new sounds – a different way* of playing instruments. The children may want to have a go at conducting – let them!

Finish with one or two contrasting songs with the children playing and singing at the same time (the songs *must* be well known). Alternatively, you could finish with a tape containing snippets of music/songs that you have selected. It is worth while considering your own *purpose-made tape.*

The following songs are suitable for this stage of percussion:

1 To the tune of 'Mulberry Bush':
We can play our rubber drums *boom, boom, boom!*
(loudly) We can play our rubber drums
(quietly) We can play our rubber drums
(quickly) We can play our rubber drums
(slowly) We can play our rubber drums.
We can play our tambourines (shakers, clappers, etc.)
2 The Band (traditional)[2 and 4]
3 The Music Makers (page 52)
4 When you beat on the drum[11]
5 The Children's Band[12]
6 Aiken Drum (adapted for instruments)[5]

Music cards When the children become more expert at handling the instruments and are used to the discipline of playing with others, start introducing music cards. These are similar in function to reading flashcards and provide a valuable *pre-reading and number activity*.

The symbol ● for one beat or strike has been suggested as a preparation for music reading. Help the children at first by pointing to each symbol and remember to move from *left to right*.

Later on introduce cards for different groups of instruments. The children also love to have a turn at holding up the cards and, as with conducting, having two independent groups responding to two sets of cards can be fun for a short time.

This training in the use of percussion can extend over the first year; perhaps into the second. It is a good introduction to group music making, accompanying songs and creative music making (see Chapter 4). The cards can be used as a prelude to word rhythm cards, but both are in the nature of pre-(music) reading activities.

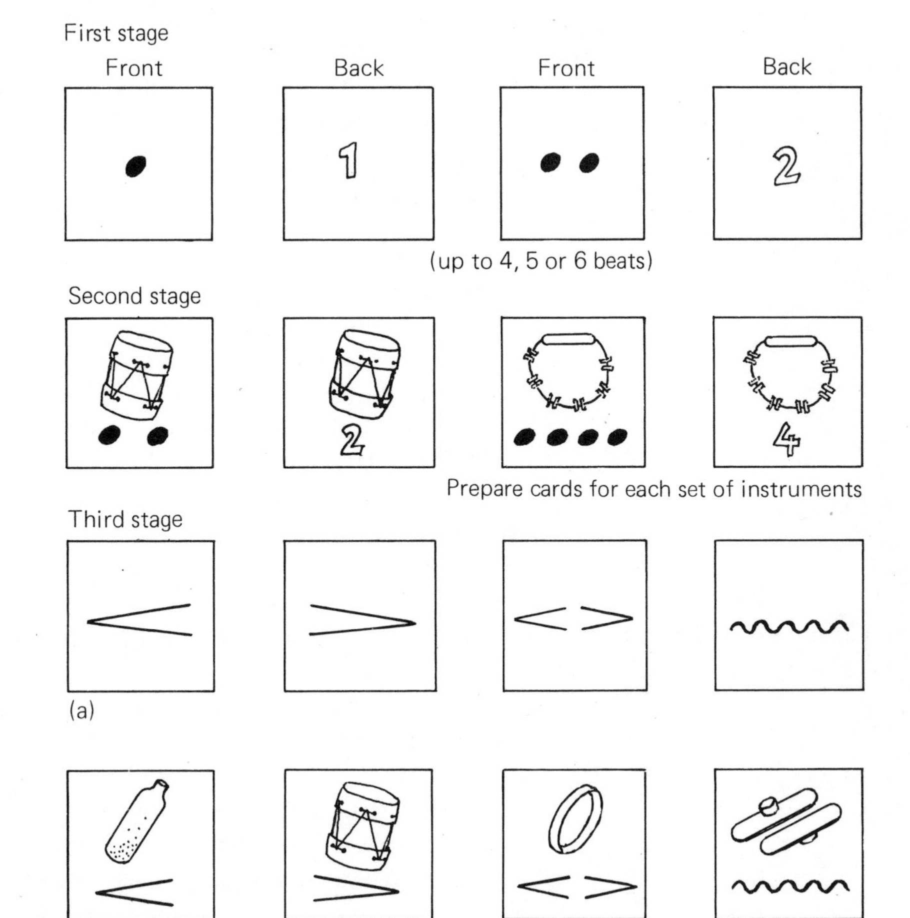

USING PERCUSSION INSTRUMENTS WITH SONGS

We can use percussion instruments with songs and singing games to:

(a) accompany songs about *instruments* (see page 48)
(b) play on the *chorus* (see page 41)
(c) accompany *actions*, for example:

London Bridge is falling down[4]
The Happy Workmen (page 52)
Counting Song (page 54)
If you're happy and you know it[1]
Everybody do this[2]
Join in the game[2]

(d) accompany specific *sound words* or phrases, adding atmosphere and often playing non-rhythmically, for example:

Rain, Hail, Snow (page 53)
The Little Red Bus[6]
There was an Old Witch[1]
Wiggley Woo (page 55)
Counting Song (page 54)
The Little Pig (page 57)
Jingle at the Windows (page 56)
The Postman (page 58)

(e) add a *general accompaniment* to songs that lend themselves to rhythmic percussion, for example:

Cumbaya[13]
Hie Dee Roon (calypso) (page 59)
Michael Finnigin[1]
Morning Town Ride[1]
Yellow Submarine[1]
Train is a-coming[1]
Jamaica Farewell[6]

This order roughly represents a progression in the use of instruments.

Choosing and using the material

Songs for percussion with younger children should be short and very simple with repetitive words or a good chorus; in many cases you can go on adding verses to use with different instruments. It is best to let the children choose their own way of accompanying at first. Some children play on the beat; others tap out the words. The important thing is to keep the learning situation very relaxed and your percussion sessions regular.

Begin adding percussion very simply, taking care not to drown the song: give instruments to one or two children only and let the others play 'pretend' instruments. Some songs are more boisterous and can tolerate slightly more percussion accompaniment, while chorus songs can allow for even greater participation.

Older children are ready for longer songs and, with a background of early training, should be able to manage more controlled playing and the specific rhythms that form the basis for general accompaniments. These can often be based on the rhythm of a short phrase or repeat words taken from the song itself: always consider the character and mood of the song, as these examples illustrate.

'Jamaica Farewell'
This calypso-style song could be accompanied on maracas by the rhythm based on the first line:

Down the way where the nights are gay (and) Down . . .

'Train is a-coming'
The song represents a train journey and should have a regular 'chuffa' kind of rhythm using sand-blocks, shakers, or a brush on a drum throughout:

adjusting to the speed of the different verses. Over and above this you could use atmospheric sounds – whistle for 'The train is a-leaving', vocal sounds for the brakes at the end and the hiss of the engine.

'Michael Finnigin'
Change the percussion on each verse to support the humour:
Use the rhythm from the name and played at half speed!

Verse 2: tambourine
Verse 3: triangle
Verse 3: guiro
Verse 4: Improvise – he grew fat and then grew thin agin!

The music makers from *Listen to the Band*

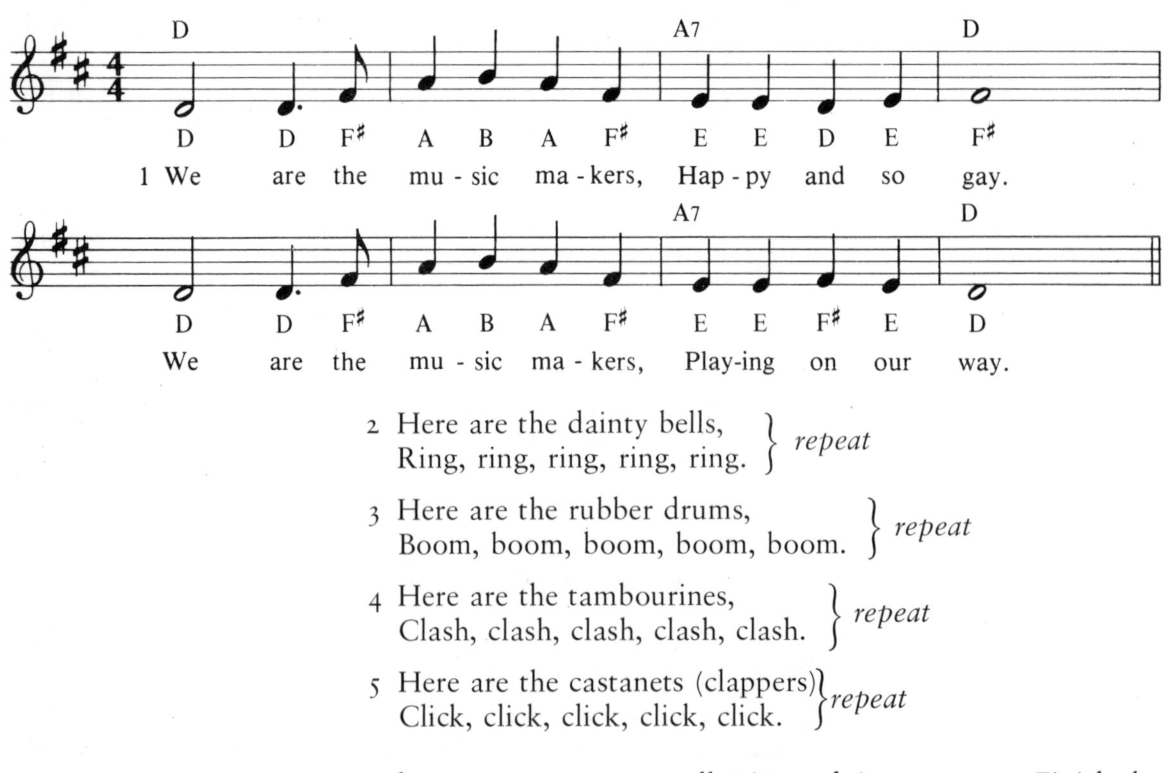

2 Here are the dainty bells,
Ring, ring, ring, ring, ring. } *repeat*

3 Here are the rubber drums,
Boom, boom, boom, boom, boom. } *repeat*

4 Here are the tambourines,
Clash, clash, clash, clash, clash. } *repeat*

5 Here are the castanets (clappers)
Click, click, click, click, click. } *repeat*

Adapt to your own collection of instruments. Finish by repeating verse 1.

The happy workmen by Mildred Logan from *Follow my Leader*

2 Rat tat rat-a-tat all day long . . .
Hear the postman sing his song . . .

3 Rum tum tum-te-tum all day long . . .
Hear the drummer sing his song . . .

4 Left, right, left, right, all day long . . .
Hear the soldier sing his song . . .

Percussion
Verse 1: clappers or hand castanets
Verse 2: tambour
Verse 3: rubber drum
Verse 4: school drum

The children can suggest other workmen to sing about and choose suitable percussion. This song is good as a singing game (use hats!) and for general movement.

Rain, hail, snow from *Listen to the Band*

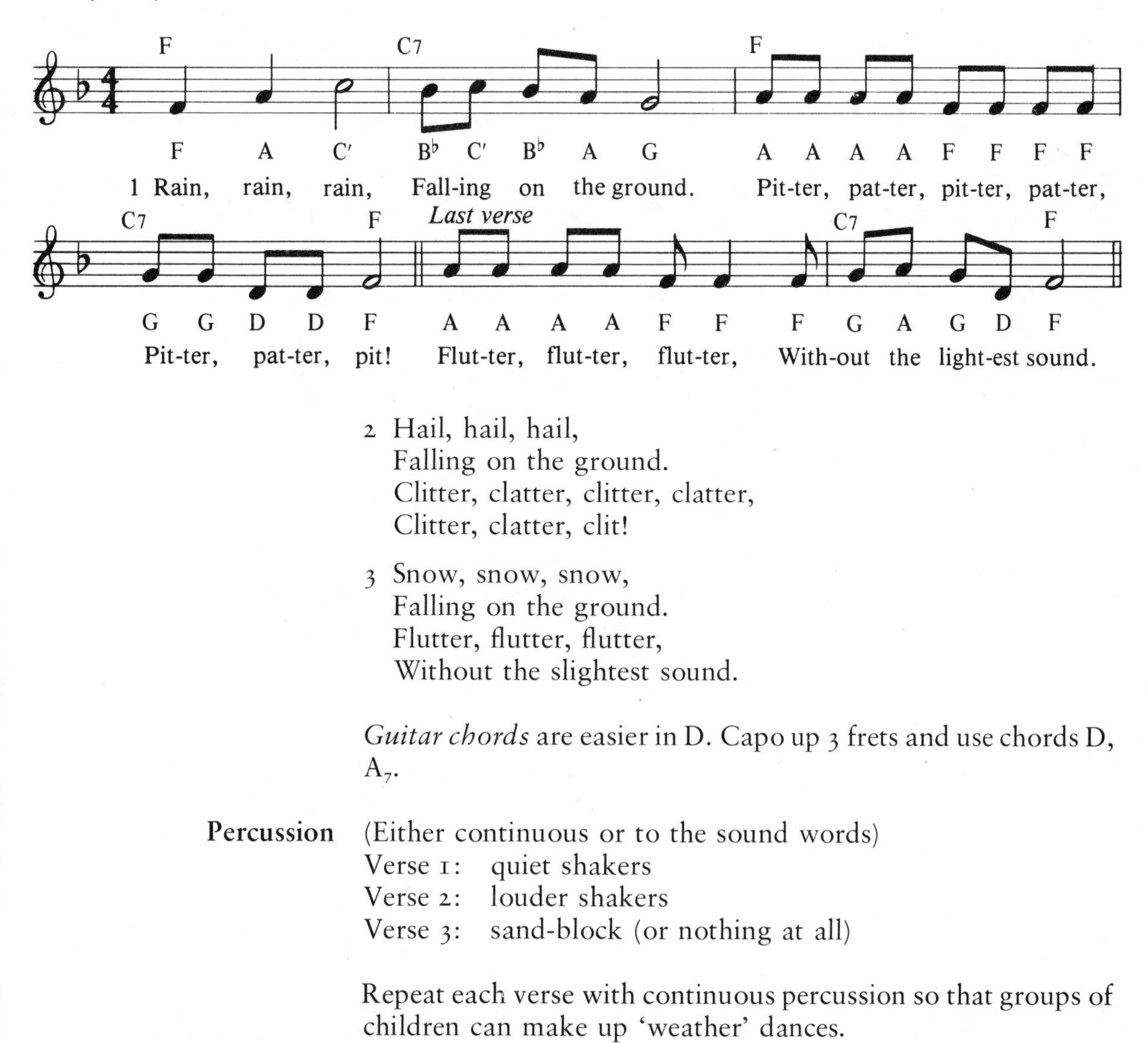

2 Hail, hail, hail,
Falling on the ground.
Clitter, clatter, clitter, clatter,
Clitter, clatter, clit!

3 Snow, snow, snow,
Falling on the ground.
Flutter, flutter, flutter,
Without the slightest sound.

Guitar chords are easier in D. Capo up 3 frets and use chords D, A_7.

Percussion (Either continuous or to the sound words)
Verse 1: quiet shakers
Verse 2: louder shakers
Verse 3: sand-block (or nothing at all)

Repeat each verse with continuous percussion so that groups of children can make up 'weather' dances.

Counting song

Words and music by Wendy van Blankenstein

2 Let's collect conkers all shiny and brown,
Look for the prickles that fall to the ground,
Scuff the leaves over so crispy and gold,
Then pick up the conkers, they're lovely to hold.
Chorus

3 Can I have sixpence to go to the shops?
One, two, three, four, five, six pennies I've got,
But sixpence in pennies doesn't last long,
Six, five, four, three, two, one, now they're all gone.
Chorus

Guitar chords are easier in D. Capo up 3 frets and use chords D, A_7.

Adapt the first verse for all the fruit trees the children know.

Percussion Shakers on the last line of verse one; clappers on the chorus.

Singing game Children stand in a circle, one in the centre as a tree. Mime the verses and walk or skip round on the chorus.

Wiggley Woo

Traditional
from *Sing-a-Song-One*

2 There's a worm at the bottom of my garden,
And his name is Wiggley Woo.
There's a worm at the bottom of my garden,
And all that he can do
Is wiggle along and wiggle around
And wiggle himself back under the ground,
There's a worm at the bottom of my garden,
And his name is Wiggley Woo.

Guitar chords are easier in D. Capo up 3 frets and use chords D, A_7, E_7, and G.

Percussion Use the framework of the first verse to make up some more verses about animals and/or pets:

> There's a snail at the bottom of my garden
> And his name is Slithery Sid . . . (sand-block)
> Freddie Frog . . . (clappers)
> Hoppity Hare . . . (tambourine)

Movement Use the percussion you have chosen to accompany the children's movement, or they could work in pairs accompanying one another.

Jingle at the windows

Traditional
from *American Folk Songs for Children*

Percussion Use a tambourine, shaker or bells to accompany the words 'Jingle at the windows' and throughout the chorus.

Singing game The children stand in a circle with hands joined and arms raised to make windows.

One, two or three children are chosen to stand outside the circle. On each 'Pass – windows', they go in, out and in again through different windows, then stand in front of a partner at 'Jingle at the windows'.

They make up a clapping chorus dance with their partners, everyone joining in clapping, then the game starts again with the children chosen as partners going outside the circle.

The little pig

Traditional
Words adapted from song in *American Folk Songs for Children*

2 Now that little pig curled up in a heap,
Oink, oink, oink,
That little pig curled up in a heap,
He joined his friends and went to sleep
Oink, oink, oink.

3 They slept and slept and slept and slept,
Sh-sh-sh-
They slept and slept and slept and slept
And slept and slept and slept and slept –
Sh-sh-sh-

4 The farmer woke them one by one,
Oink, oink, oink,
The farmer woke them one by one
And then they rolled out in the sun,
Oink, oink, oink.

5 They rolled and rolled and rolled and rolled . . .
(The music of this stanza may be repeated *ad lib.*)

6 Those little pigs rolled back in their pen,
Oink, oink, oink,
Those little pigs rolled back in their pen
And then they went to sleep again,
Oink, oink, oink.

Percussion Verse 2: shakers; Verse 3: sand-blocks; Verse 4: clappers; Verses 5 and 6: shakers

Finish by humming and accompany with sand-blocks.

The postman

by Edwards Hughes
from *People who Help Us*

Percussion Clappers or wood-blocks on the 'Rat-a-tat's. Choose a different sound for 'Plop-plop-plop'. Can the children make the 'Rat-a-tat's *louder* in the second verse.

Make up some verses about tradesmen who come down the street making a noise and choose suitable percussion:

dustman (bang, bang, bang!)
ice-cream van (ting-a-ling-ling!)

Hie dee roon

Jamaican calypso song
from *Music Education in the Primary School*

1 Show me your dancing,
  Hie dee roon, oh . . .

2 Show me your clapping,
  Hie dee roon, oh . . .

Many more verses can be added in this way. Make up words for a Christmas calypso:

Christmas is coming,
Clap your hands . . .

Guitar chords are easier in D. Capo up 3 frets and use chords D, A_7.

Percussion Use a tambourine or maracas to accompany the rhythm of the words 'Hie dee roon, oh' throughout.

TUNED PERCUSSION

Chimebars, xylophone, glockenspiel and metallophone are the most common pitched instruments used in schools, but suggestions in this section can apply to most pitched instruments, which can be used in a number of ways.

Sound effects

(a) A clock chiming (as in 'Hickory Dickory Dock').
(b) A short continuous glissando (slide) on the xylophone gives a good 'purr'; use with 'Pussy cat, pussy cat, where have you been?'
(c) A series of quiet notes on the chimes or glock will give an effect of twinkling stars; use with 'Twinkle, twinkle, little star'.
(d) As used in sound pictures (Chapter 4).

Making up tunes

See Chapter 4.

Song accompaniments

Before using any instruments for accompanying songs, make sure that your children have had plenty of practice using body sounds and unpitched percussion, and handling the instruments in the music corner on their own.

Make sure that each child knows how to *play* the instrument, how to relax the arm and wrist and how to bounce off the middle part of the note. This will come with informal practice, but I have found it useful to use chimebars (one for each child) with a suitably small group in this way:

1. All play together, keeping time with a slowish beat.
2. Individual children play 2, 3, 4 (hold up fingers or flashcards).
3. Each child plays and sings the name of his chimebar: 'My chimebar is called G.' (Darken the letter already inscribed on the metal bar – either permanently with paint or temporarily with pencil.) Everyone sings back.
4. Each child plays his chimebar when the note name is called. Try calling a tune snippet if you can, like E D G – 'Three Blind Mice'.

The children should know the song well before they begin to add an accompaniment.

All children should have an opportunity of accompanying songs if they wish. This is easier if you sing informally, fairly often and if the instruments are accessible!

As well as teaching accompaniments, allow your children to try devising some of their own. Start off by giving them the notes (chimebars are good for this) and as much help as they need. Encourage their own efforts as they gain confidence.

Ostinati Ostinato accompaniment is the simplest form of tune accompaniment. The word 'ostinato' simply means a little tune or fragment of a tune that keeps repeating itself and can comprise just one note, called a *drone*, or two, three, or four *note patterns*.

They can form a delightful accompaniment to songs and rounds based on simple harmony and, taught by rote, give the young player an immediate sense of achievement.

Playing by ear Most children love picking out a tune that they know; they derive great satisfaction from the act of producing it themselves. Simple workcards can help to start them off and provide a valuable aid in both reading and listening.

It is best to begin with tune snippets that the children know really well and with reception children workcards like these, used with chimebars, can provide a matching activity as well, if the drawings are done to size. (Note: C′ is top C, C is bottom C.)

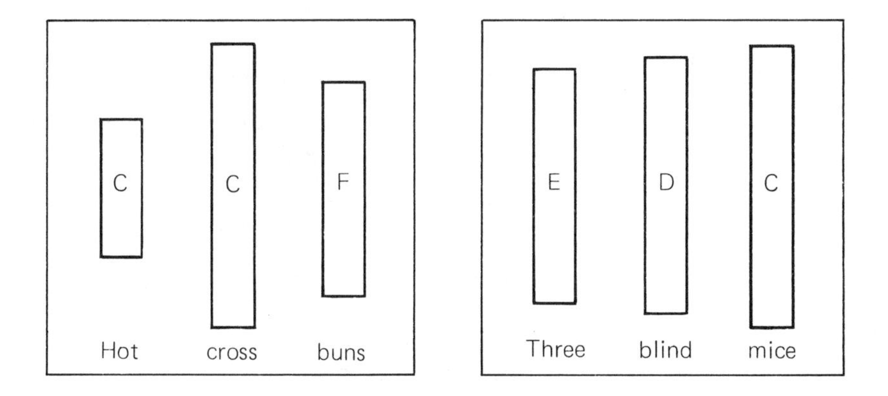

Other suitable snippets for younger children to use with diagram workcards are given below.

C F
London's burning (page 65)

E D C
Moo Moo Moo (from 'I went to visit a farm one day'[4])

C E G
Tommy Thumb[4]

C′ A F
Roll over (from 'There were ten in the bed'[2], page 64)

F A C′
Rain rain rain (from 'Rain, hail, snow', page 53)

F A C′
Puffer train[4]

E C
Tick Tock (ostinato for 'Hickory Dickory Dock', page 64)

C E G
Pat-a-cake (from 'Pat-a-cake, pat-a-cake, baker's man'[4])

C′ A F
Old woman (from 'Old woman, old woman won't you come a-shearing'[1])

C′ A F
Aeroplanes (from 'Aeroplane, aeroplanes all in a row'[4])

Progress to longer snippets and just write in the note names:

E F G G A B C′
Hickory Dickory Dock

C E E E E D C C C
I went to visit a farm one day[4]

E G A E G
Train whistle blowing[1]

G A G E C
In middle ocean[1]

G G A G E C
Five little speckled frogs[1]

C C F F F F
There were ten in the bed

G A B D D E G
There's a hole in my bucket[1]

G G E F G E
My ship sailed from China[1]

G E E E D E F E
The bear went over the mountain[1]

C F G A B♭ C′ C′ C′ B♭ A
There was a man who had a horselum[1]

These snippets are the beginnings of songs, and many children will eventually go on to complete the songs themselves. Help them by making the relevant chimebar notes available, or by taking off the ones they won't need if they are using a xylophone or glockenspiel with loose notes. Small glocks are not really suitable for this activity.

Further reading

Many suggestions for stories with **sound effects** will be found in *Growing Up with Music* (page 5) by Mary Pape (Oxford University Press, 1970); *Musical Merry-Go-Round* by Robina Beckles Wilson (Heinemann, 1977); *Ready to Play: Stories with percussion sounds* by James Blades and Carole Ward (BBC Publications, 1978); *Sing-a-Song One* and *Sing-a-Song Two* by Wendy Bird and Gary McAuliffe (Nelson, 1978).

The following books give more suggestions on the use of **ostinati**: *Ring-a-Ding* and *Ding-Dong Bell* by Yvonne Adair (Novello, 1962); *Rhymes with Chimes* by Olive Rees and Anne Mendoza (Oxford University Press, 1959); *Seventy Simple Songs with Ostinati* by Albert Chatterley (Novello, 1969); *Tops and Tails, More Tops and Tails* and *Tops and Tails Again* by Anne Mendoza (Oxford University Press, 1968).

OSTINATI

Using 1 note

You can use a different note for accompanying, so long as it is not too high or too low, and sing accordingly. (Choose from E, F, G, A.)

Using 2 notes

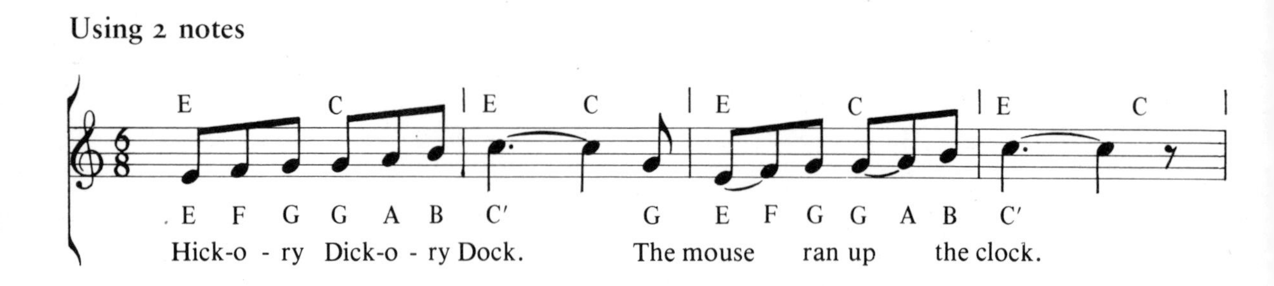

The ostinato can represent the clock ticking. These notes do not on their own fit 'The clock struck one, the mouse ran down', but the 'ticks' should go right on to the end. A small group could sing 'tick-tock' with the chimes.

F C F C | F C F C | F C F C | F C F C
F C F A B♭ G A F F C C F A B♭ G A F
Ding Dong Bell, Pus-sy's in the well! Who put her in? Lit-tle Tom-my Green.
F C | F C | F C | F C
F G A F F G A F A B♭ C′ A B♭ C′
Frè - re Jac - ques, Frè - re Jac-ques, Dor - mez vous? Dor - mez vous?
F F F | C C C
C F F F F A C′ A F G G G E D
The wheels on the bus go round and round, round and round, round and
F F F | C C F
C C F F F F A C′ A F G C F
round. The wheels on the bus go round and round, all day long.
F F C | F F C
F F F A C′ G F F G E C C
Jump! Jump! Kan-ga-roo Brown. Jump! Jump! Off to town.
F F C | F F C F
F F F A C′ G F F G E C F
Jump! Jump! Up hill and down. Jump! Jump! Kan - ga - roo Brown.
C | F F C | F F C | F F C | F F
C C F F C C F F G G A A G G A A
Lon-don's burn-ing, Lon-don's burn - ing, Fetch the en - gines, Fetch the en - gines.

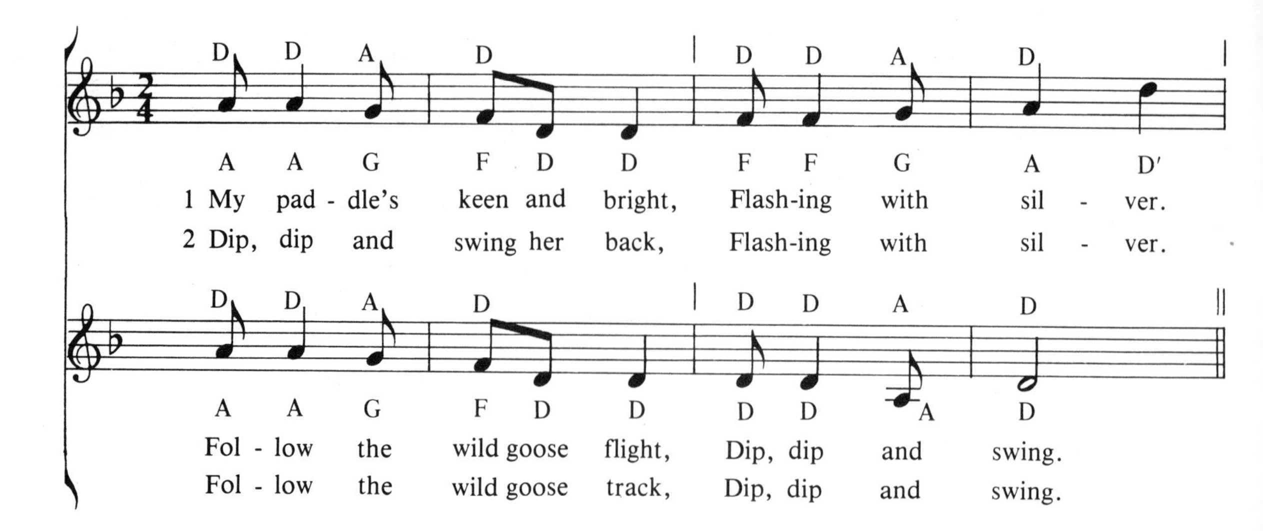

The A in this ostinato *can* be a high A, though a low A sounds better and of course matches the tune to the words 'Dip, dip and swing'. A small group could sing these words with the chimes.

Using 3 or more notes

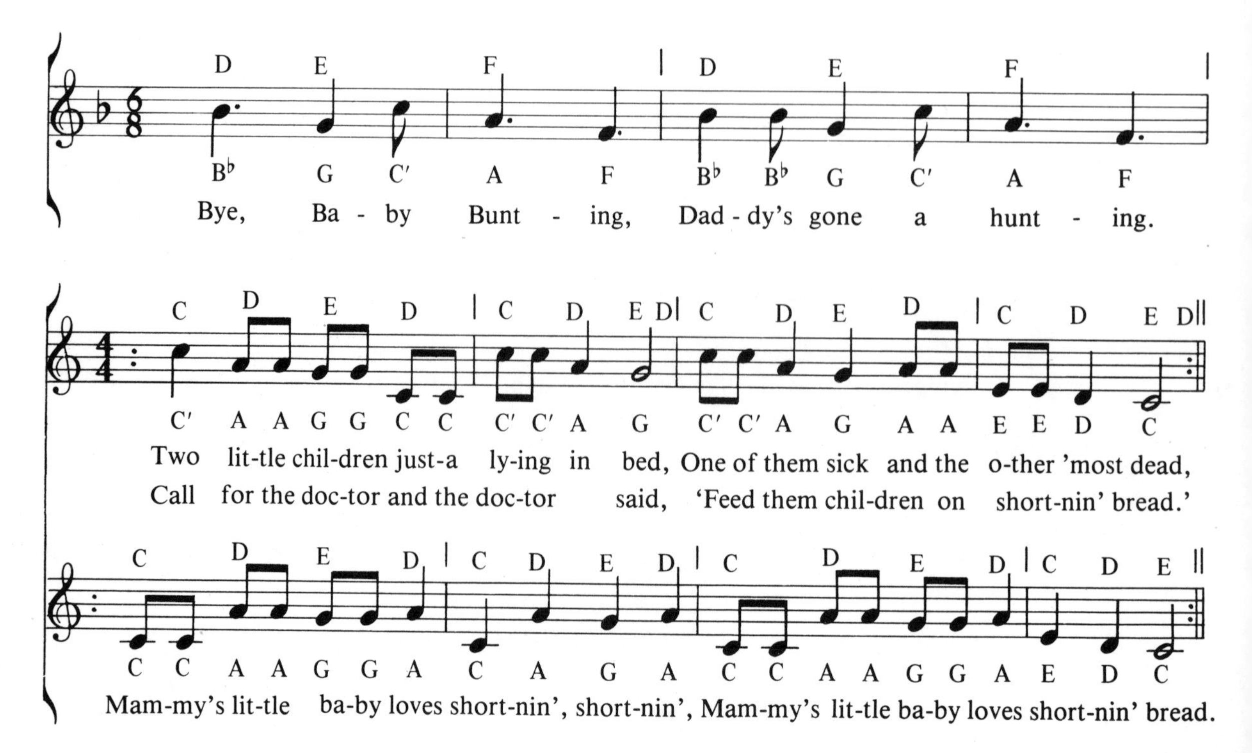

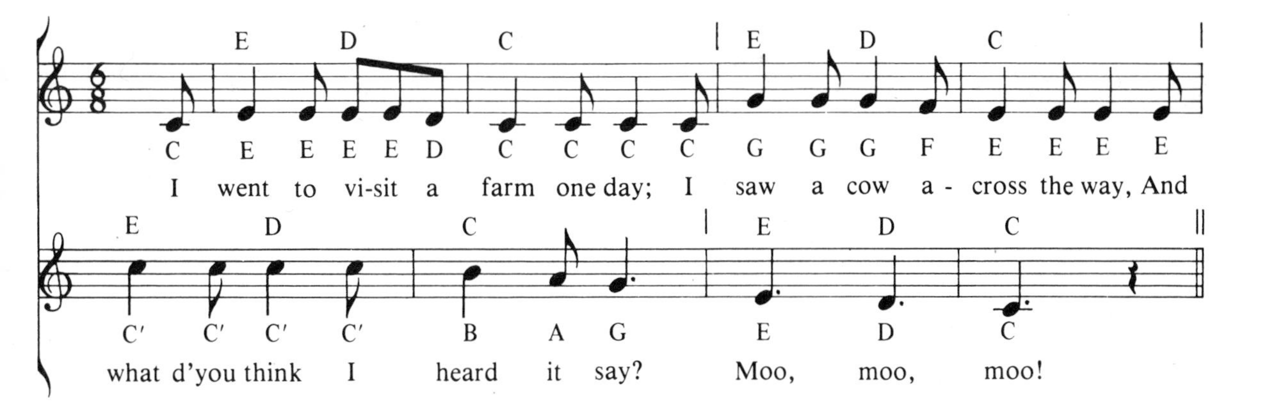

A small group could sing with the ostinato 'Moo, moo, moo!'

A small group could sing with the ostinato 'Hot Cross Buns!'

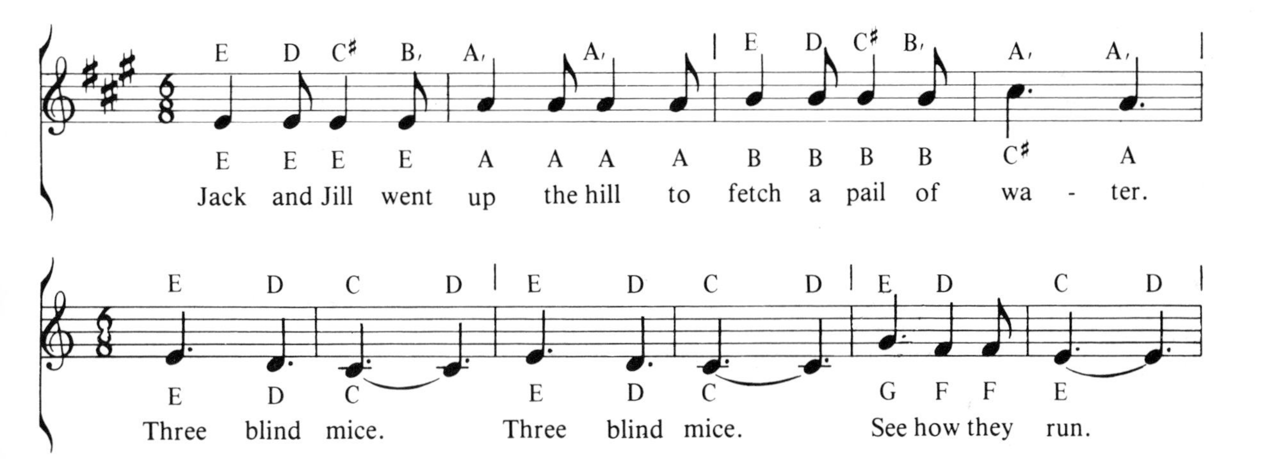

4 EXPLORING SOUND

For the children this is probably one of the first starting points in their own music making; they are natural explorers and will enjoy experimenting with sound makers as soon as they encounter an inviting music corner. In the playground they will use their voices freely in their dramatic play: 'boom-boom', 'zzz . . .', 'swish-swish' as they ride around, soar up in their activities that they will be able to go on to improvise or create by use of sound by providing *opportunities, suitable materials*, and *direction*, just as we do in art to help the young painter. Listening and singing games, percussion playing and handling instruments in the music corner will help the children to discriminate and to choose instruments that will give the most suitable sound to accompany their actions or express their feelings – shakers for rain, a drum for a soldier, perhaps a cymbal for something frightening. They will learn how to handle instruments and the different ways of playing – loud, quiet, quick, slow, trilling, shaking, beating – so that they will have experience of producing a greater *range* of sound. It is only when they have taken part in a variety of directed music-making activities that they will be able to go on to improvise or create by themselves. The suggestions for group work contained in this chapter therefore should not be attempted until the children have had some experience of the approaches outlined in the first part of this book.

PICTURES, STORIES AND PATTERNS IN SOUND

Here are some possible lines of development:

1 One sound = one thing; sounds can heighten dramatic play; they can accompany very simple verses, rhymes and action songs.
2 Several sounds can be sequenced together to form a narrative.
3 Sounds can accompany a poem or story.
4 Several sounds can be patterned together by the children *working in groups* to suggest an event, a happening, the core of a story, even an impression or feeling. Responding first to the teacher's direction, they will learn how to work with

their friends, re-creating the music they have helped to make or working out their own ideas.

The following subjects lend themselves to interpretation in sound:

Weather – rain, hail, snow, fog, mist, a thunderstorm.

Machines – a clock shop, a factory, daleks, robots, vehicles.

Water – under the sea, fish, an aquarium, the seaside.

Air – birds, butterflies, insects, a space journey.

Events – Hallowe'en, a fair, a circus, a train journey, a busy station, shopping in the High Street.

Impressions – can be about anything – night; day; moods; feelings – as well as fantasy creatures and fantasy worlds.

Stories, songs, radio and television programmes will provide many more suitable starting points. The important thing is to *recognize opportunities* when they present themselves as well as to refrain from forcing this kind of activity when the material available is just not suitable, when the timing is not right or when the children are not ready.

How to organize

The most suitable way is to sit with the children in a circle as suggested in the approach to percussion work; exploring sound is, in fact, an extension of this aspect of music making. Choose a carpeted area if you can or use a P.E. mat to display the instruments you are going to use. There should be an instrument for every child, but, if not, some children can contribute body or vocal sounds where suitable. Some teachers might prefer to start by using fewer instruments and more body sounds.

Display some good pictures if you can and tell the children what you are going to do: 'We are going to make some music about the wind . . .'. Talk about the various sounds that are involved (a valuable time for language development) and let the children sit together according to the type of sound they choose to make; do this quickly, let them choose their instruments and begin practising straight away. This will be noisy so use a visual signal for stopping them. Then listen to each group of sounds at a time. Discuss and, if necessary, suggest improvements (not for too long) and have one more short practice. Explain briefly how you are going to ask them to play – in what order, etc. – and then conduct the children by pointing to groups or individuals to start playing and use another signal (holding up hands) to stop them. At a later stage a child could conduct. Make several different sound pictures by altering the sequence of sounds and encourage the children to vary their playing as you have taught them in group percussion sessions – loud, quiet, quick, slow, short, long. Aim at some kind of *overall pattern* – an important principle of musical composition that can be introduced even at this early age.

Follow up this activity by:

(a) leaving the instruments in the *music corner* together with a suitable picture for small group work (two, three, or four children);
(b) encouraging the children to write stories or draw pictures;
(c) providing opportunities for painting and/or craft;
(d) linking with movement where suitable.

Here are some suggestions for exploring sound with the children, together with relevant poems and listening music. The suggestions for instruments or sound makers in this book should be used only as an initial guide – the children will have many ideas of their own.

A rainy day

Sound sequence

Story line	*Suggested sound makers*
The children go out with their mothers to the park,	clappers or rhythm sticks (walking pace)
but it begins to rain.	shakers or bells (light rain)
They put on their coats and hurry home as the rain gets heavier.	clappers/rhythm sticks (running pace) shakers or bells (light rain) add tambourines (heavy rain)
They listen to the rain on the windows when they get home.	a tapped triangle or tapped bells
Afterwards the house and the garden are dripping wet. Then the sun comes out.	'drips' from any tapped instrument gentle chimes

Poems

Who likes the rain[15]
There was a young lady of Spain[16]
Pitter-patter[17]
Rain on the house-top[17]

Rain Sizes
Rain comes in various sizes,
Some rain is small as a mist.
It tickles your face with surprises,
And tingles as if you'd been kissed.

Some rain is the size of a sprinkle
And doesn't put out the sun,
You can see the drops sparkle and twinkle,
And a rainbow comes out when it's done.

Some rain is as big as a nickel,
And comes with a crash and a hiss.
It comes down too heavy to tickle.
It's more like a splash than a kiss.

When it rains the right size and you're wrapped in
Your rainclothes, it's fun out of doors.
But run home before you get trapped in
The big rain that rattles and roars.
John Ciardi

Songs
Pray open your umbrella
Pray open your umbrella
Pray open your umbrella,
And shield me from the rain.

The shower is nearly over,
The shower is nearly over,
The shower is nearly over
So shut it up again.

(The tune can be found in *This Little Puffin* and *Fingers and Thumbs*.)

To the tune of 'In and Out the Windows':

See the rain come pouring down,
Cleaning up the dirty town,
Filling all the gutters full,
As the children go to school.

Chorus:
Paddling in the puddles,
Paddling in the puddles,
Paddling in the puddles,
But don't let mummy see! (whisper)
Wendy van Blankenstein

Pitter-patter[19]
It's raining[20]
Rain, hail, snow (page 53)

Listening
'Gardens in the rain' by Debussy

Night **Sound poems**

Someone	*Suggested percussion*
Someone came knocking At my wee, small door; Someone came knocking, I'm sure – sure – sure;	quiet clappers or a 'clamped' triangle
I listened, I opened, I looked to left and right, But nought there was a-stirring In the still dark night;	gentle rasp or guiro
Only the busy beetle Tap-tapping in the wall,	wood-block or rhythm stick
Only from the forest The screech owl's call;	muted voice (as if owl is a long way away)
Only the cricket whistling	voice
While the dewdrops fall, So I know not who came knocking At all, at all, at all. *Walter de la Mare*	gentle chime or glock.

Noises in the Night	*Suggested percussion*
When I'm in bed at night, All tucked up warm and tight, All kinds of noises Go in at my two ears.	
Brr . . . go the motor cars	sandpaper-blocks
Out in the street.	shakers
Whirr . . . sings the wind.	voices
Ting-a-ling-ling Ring the bicycle bells	triangle
And ding-dong, ding-dong Sings the Grandfather clock downstairs. Then I hear nothing – nothing at all, Because I'm asleep, sound asleep. *Lilian McCrea*	chimebars

Encourage the children to listen to sounds that they can hear outside their houses at night. Swop experiences the next day; get the children to match up the remembered sounds on instruments or other sound makers. Make a recording yourself one night and ask the children to identify the sounds.

Hiawatha's Boyhood
At the door on summer evenings
Sat the little Hiawatha;
Heard the whispering of the pine trees,
Heard the lapping of the water. . . .

An evocative night picture is contained in this part of the *Hiawatha* ballad.

'Things that go "bump" in the night' by Spike Milligan[23]

Song
'Night Piece'[22]

Listening
Nocturnes by Chopin (calm)
Night on the Bare Mountain by Mussorgsky (exciting)

Butterflies **Sound poems**

Butterflies
All day long in the garden
Are butterflies flitting by,
White, pale yellow, and orange bright
And some like the blue of the sky.
Clive Sansom

Sound picture
The children can imitate the flight of the butterfly on suitable instruments. Then let them choose different instruments for the four colours and play in four groups, the sounds in each group coming and going, stopping and starting, playing slowly, quickly, loudly, quietly. They must listen carefully to vary the playing of their own instrument within their own group. Organize this yourself to start with, then let one of the children do the conducting.

Hallowe'en **Sound picture** suggesting an event and possibly linked with a story, e.g. 'The Once-a Year Witch' by J. Varga (Pergamon Press, 1974).

A witch's kitchen	*Suggested sound makers*
Wind	voices – *oo-oos* sung at different pitches – going up and down – getting loud, then quiet again
Cauldron crackling	shakers; crumpled newspaper
Witch laughing	voice
Spell	a slide on the xylophone followed by a few notes on the chimes or glock
Frog	clappers, sticks or wood-block
Spider	gentle slides on guiro, rasp or wooden washboard

The chart below suggests one arrangement, but virtually any combination and order of sounds will make an interesting composition. Try several; tape them and discuss the results.

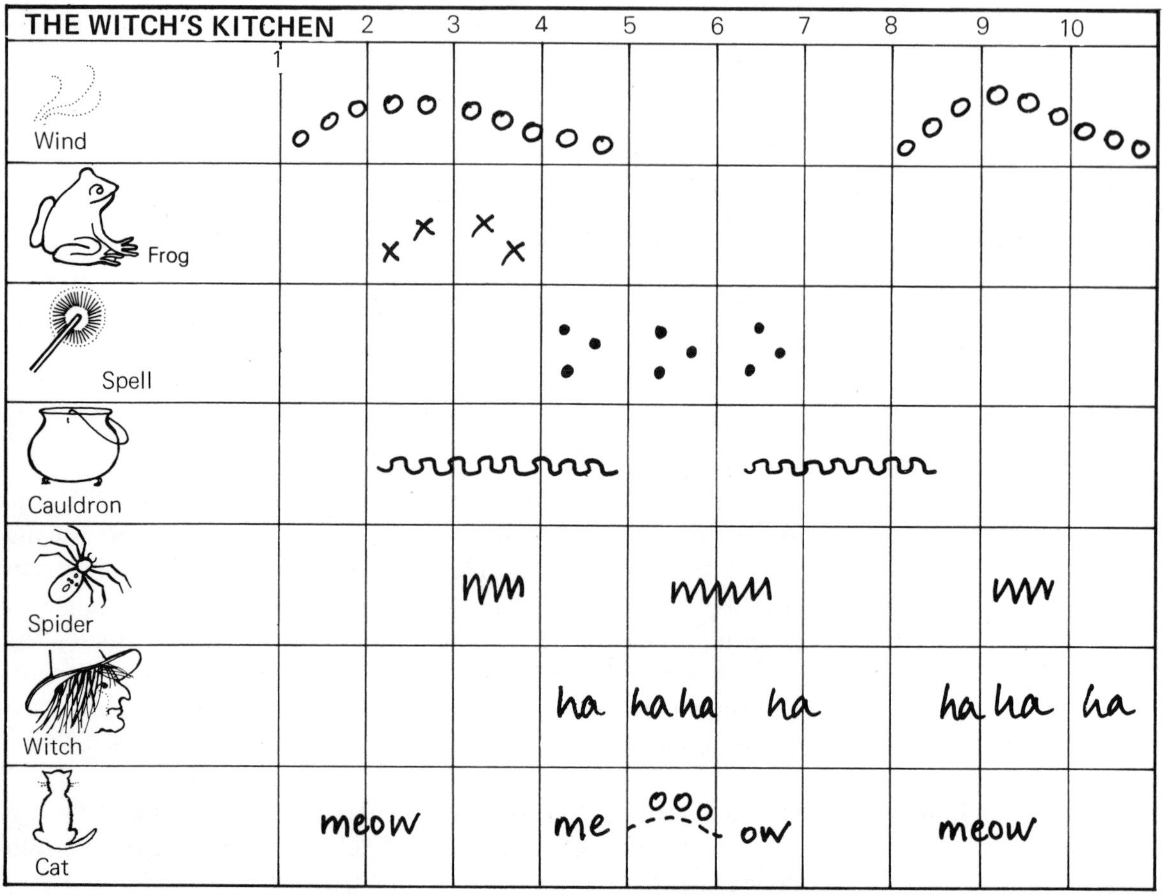

THE WITCH'S KITCHEN	1	2	3	4	5	6	7	8	9	10
Wind										
Frog										
Spell										
Cauldron										
Spider										
Witch				ha	haha	ha		ha	ha	ha
Cat	meow			me	ooo	ow		meow		

Poems

Heigh ho! for Hallowe'en.
All the witches to be seen,
Some black and some green,
Heigh ho! for Hallowe'en.
(Anon)

There was an old witch,
Believe it if you can,
She tapped on the window,
And she ran, ran, ran.
She ran helter-skelter,
With her toes in the air,
Cornstalks flying
From the old witch's hair.

'Swish' goes the broomstick,
'Meow' goes the cat,
'Plop' goes the hop toad
Sitting on her hat.
'Wee' chuckled I,
'What fun, fun, fun!'
Hallowe'en night
When the witches run.
(Words traditional)

Hallowe'en[24] by Leonard Clark
Shadows and Spells[25]
'Witch Witch' by Rose Fyleman[23]
'The Ride by Nights' by Walter de la Mare[26]
'The Witches' Chant' by William Shakespeare[26]

Songs

Weather Witch[20]
Hallowe'en[27]
Hallowe'en is coming[5]
Witch Song[5]
There was an old witch[1]
Skin and Bones[6]
Witches of Hallowe'en[28]
Hallowe'en Coming[7]

Stories

The Once-a-Year Witch
Meg and Mog[6]
The Good Bad Witch[28]

Listening

'In the Hall of the Mountain King' from *Peer Gynt* Suite by Grieg

Hänsel and Gretel by Humperdinck

The Wind

Sound picture

Choose a windy day to focus on local gusty sounds; encourage the children to think of phrases to describe what they have seen, felt or heard on a windy day. Assemble some ideas and shape them into a class tone poem. Write it down and get the children to accompany their poem with suitable sounds.

Poems

The following is a good poem to inspire creative writing on this theme, or use it as a sound poem with younger children.

Wind Song	*Suggested percussion*
When the wind blows	
The quiet things speak.	whispering
Some whisper, some clang,	a clapper
Some creak.	quiet 'rasp'
Grasses swish.	voices
Treetops sigh.	voices
Flaps slap	a clap
and snap at the sky.	clappers
Wires on poles	
whistle and hum	voices
Ashcans roll.	tambourine
Windows drum.	drum

When the wind goes –
suddenly
then,
the quiet things
are quiet again.
Lilian Moore

'Windy Nights' by Robert Louis Stevenson[29]
'When the wind is in the east'[30]
'The Wind' by James Reeves[31]

Alternatively this poem invites a more rhythmic accompaniment:

Windy Nights	*Suggested accompaniment*
Rumbling in the chimneys,	drum
Rattling at the doors	tambourine
Round the roofs and round the roads	low chimebar
The rude wind roars;	
Raging through the darkness,	drum
Raving through the trees,	tambourine
Racing off again across	drum and tambourine
The great grey seas	gradually getting quieter
Rodney Bennett	

Create your own sound picture of the wind, using ideas from these and other poems and from the children.

	Suggested sound makers
Wind	voices (ooo—)
Telephone wires humming	voices (mmm—)
Trees blowing	shakers
Gate banging	clappers
Dustbin lid rolling along	cymbal (or saucepan and spoon – even a dustbin lid)
Paper-bags being blown along	paper (tissue, newspaper, etc.)
Washing flapping on the line	flap a small piece of material or sheet of newspaper

Suggested arrangement

The sound of the wind and telephone wires humming can be in the background all the time. They can suddenly increase to represent a gust of wind and the 'gust' can be followed by one or two of the suggested sounds. The wind can die down at the end. Thus the pattern would be:

Wind and telephone wires sound – a gust of wind is followed by a gate banging and a line of washing flapping. The wind dies down, then a further gust is followed by a dustbin lid clanking along, etc. Finish with the voices of the wind and the wires gradually getting quieter and quieter until they stop altogether.

Using a visual 'score' (see below) is another way of conducting a sound picture. When the children are ready to play, move your finger, or a pointer very slowly *from left to right*. The children play when the pointer reaches their bit and stop when it moves on. You can move your finger back if you want to extend or continue a part; you can play right through several times in different ways – going quickly/slowly, playing loudly/quietly, etc.

Songs

The wind blows east[5]
Falling leaves[6]
The north wind doth blow[6]
Windy old weather[32]
The mill wheel[20]
Weather witch[20]

Finger play

Five little leaves[5]

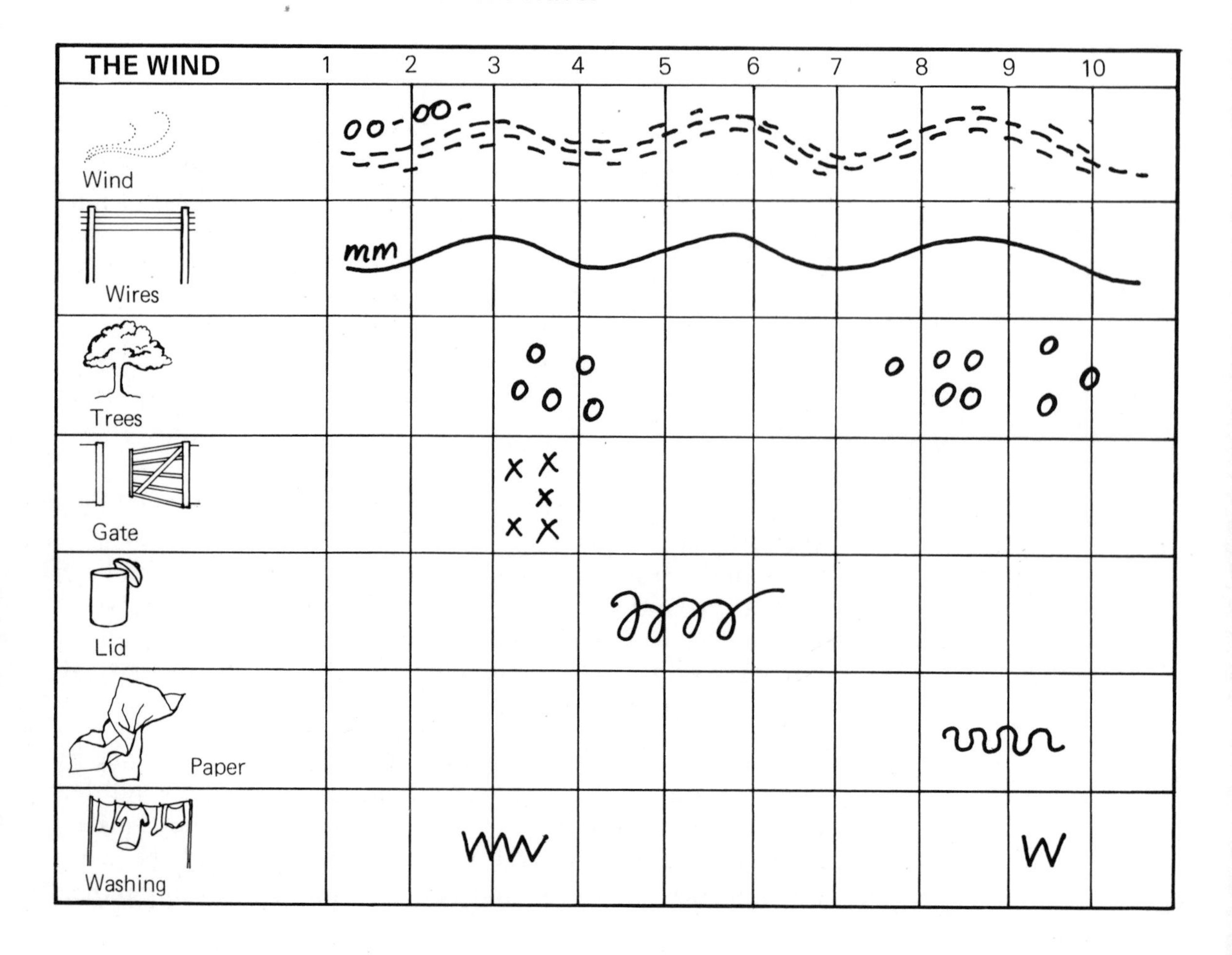

Noah's Ark

Sound sequence

The story of the Ark is a rich source of ideas for work in exploring sound and dramatic movement. It is a long narrative and with older children it is best to divide it into parts so that musical interest can be sustained through the more detailed ideas that can be encouraged this way.

Story line	*Suggested sound makers*
Part 1: Noah and his family build the ark.	
Chopping trees	clappers or wood banged with a stick
Sawing wood	a guiro, wooden washboard or corrugated card. Try different sticks for the 'saw'.
Hammering (small)	clappers (or claves)
(big)	drum or tambour
Sandpapering	sandpaper blocks
Painting	soft brush on drum or tambour head
People talking	children whispering in a group making up 'mini' conversations; occasionally a laugh directed at Noah

Part 2: The animals arrive. (This should be preceded by talking about the way different animals move and linking with movement; it could form the basis for several hall sessions. The sounds could be played one after another in a kind of procession, or there could be a build up as more and more animals approach the ark.)

Snakes, worms – 'crawlies' in general	sandpaper blocks; rustled or crumpled paper of differing textures – insides of chocolate boxes etc.
Birds, butterflies and flying creatures	bells, jingles, random notes on the glockenspiel or chimebars
Rabbits, kangaroos and creatures that hop	clappers; beats on a tambour or drum in a 'hopping' rhythm
Elephants and big lumbering animals	a drum or bass xylophone if you have one (try the effects of different beaters)

Horses, ponies, donkeys, zebras and trotting animals	coconuts – several pairs preferably, going at different speeds

(The list is endless, but it is best to agree upon specific groups and aim for a variety of sound within each group.)

The main door closes when the Ark is full.	drum

Part 3: The rain comes.

Light rain	xylophone, tapped triangle
Heavy rain	shakers, bells
Thunder	a roll on a big drum or several rubber drums are effective played with chimebar beaters
Lightning	a cymbal – use a padded beater

It is difficult to get the effect of rain *gradually* becoming faster and heavier, so allow the children time to practise. Encourage them to *listen* carefully to one another.

The rain gradually eases off.	rain sounds quieten gradually; finish with the triangle
The raven and the dove are sent out of the ark	bells; xylophone

Part 4: Noah, his family and all the animals come out of the ark.

	Repeat the animal music from Part 2 and add a 'whispering' group to represent the humans.
The rainbow	a peal of slow notes on 'glockenspiel', chimebars or, best of all, metallophone

Poems
The Young Puffin Book of Verse (Penguin 1970) has a section on 'All the animals'.

Songs
The animals went in two by two[1]
Who built the Ark[33]
One more river[34]

Listening
Carnival of the Animals by Saint-Saëns
(and see under 'Animals' in the Recorded Music Section of Appendix 2)

Machines

Sound picture

Machines at home: encourage as many children as possible to record the sounds of machines at home; do it yourself. Bring the tape to class for a guessing game. Find *sound words* and *sound makers* to match each machine:

Typewriter	*ticker, ticker, ticker, ch!*	trill a 'clamped' triangle and 'ping' it
Telephone	*br-br . . . br-br . . . br-br . . .*	corrugated tin, bottle or guiro
Egg whisk	*whirrr, whirrr, whirrr . . .*	rolled shaker (loud one) or a whisk itself!
Lawnmower	*errrrr-rr; errrrr-rr . . .*	washboard

Divide into four groups: encourage each group to establish a specific *rhythm*; practise these rhythms quick, slow, loud, quiet, high, low (if with the voice). Try the arrangement shown on the chart below, first with voices and then sound makers in as many different ways as possible:

(to the tune of 'The wheels on the bus'[4])

1 My typewriter goes ticker, ticker, ch! . . . all day long.
2 Our telephone goes br-br . . . br-br . . .
3 Mummy's egg whisk goes whirrr, whirrr, whirrr . . .
4 Daddy's lawnmower goes errrrrr-rr, errrrrr-rr . . .

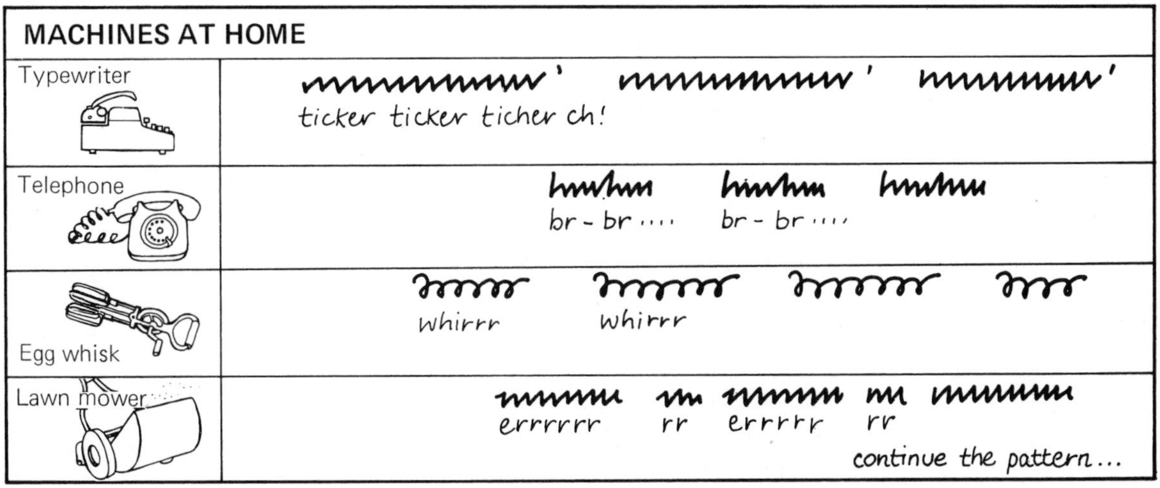

MACHINES AT HOME	
Typewriter	ticker ticker ticher ch!
Telephone	br - br .... br - br ....
Egg whisk	whirrr whirrr
Lawn mower	errrrrr rr errrrr rr continue the pattern...

Poem

Creation
The dainty old professor
Made a new machine
He built it up with dead corkscrews
And junk you've never seen,
He tied it up with chewing gum
And glued it down with strings
Then watered it with fish's milk
And many other things.
He turned it on at midnight
As the sun gained height;
He was deafened by a flash
And calmly got a fright.
The thing took down the pictures
And ironed them with a broom;
Sang 'Greensleeves' in a rusty voice
And flew about the room.

It fed the fire with stuffing
From the lounge settee;
It washed the cakes and cooked the clothes
With great alacrity.
It ate the wine and read the bread
And drank the 'Herald' dry;
It nailed some biscuits onto toast
And quietly drowned a pie.

It knocked the clock from the mantelpiece
And put some ham instead;
It sewed some tissue paper up
With cotton wire and thread.
It swept the floor with rolling pin
And brushed the lawn for fleas;
It sawed some wood with plastic comb
And climbed up all the trees.

It makes a lovely housewife, its hair is turning grey,
He wouldn't want another, in case it passed away.
Graeme Turner

Songs
Machines[35]
Wheels keep turning[1]
This is the sound our Hoover makes (to the tune of 'Mulberry Bush')

Stories

Mary Poppins in the Kitchen by P.J. Traves (Collins)
Ben in the Kitchen by Pat Albeck (Methuen)
Barbamama's Kitchen by Talus Taylor and Annette Tison (Warne)

Listening

Moving Percussion and Electronic Sound Pictures (*Listen, Move and Dance* No. 4, HMV/CLP/3531)
Perpetuum Mobile by Johann Strauss

SOUND EXPERIMENTS

Noise

I like noise.
The whoop of a boy, the thud of a hoof,
The rattle of rain on a galvanised roof,
The hubbub of traffic, the roar of a train,
The throb of machinery numbing the brain,
The switching of wires in an overhead tram,
The rush of the wind, the door on the slam,
The boom of thunder, the crash of the waves,
The din of a river that races and raves,
The crack of a rifle, the clank of a pail,
The strident tattoo of a swift-slapping sail –
From any old sound that the silence destroys
Arises a gamut of soul-stirring joys.
I like noise.
J. Pope

The nature of sound

This section outlines some basic knowledge that is helpful to have in mind when talking about sound with children, and there are a few simple experiments which the children might do. Always try out experiments yourself first so that you know they will work.

Little children will be absorbed mainly in their own efforts at *making sound*; they will be fascinated by the range of sound they can produce from the various kinds of material they can lay their hands on and they will try out different rhythms and sound effects.

1 Focus on sounds through the listening games and music-corner activities already suggested.
2 Provide for the making of some simple percussion instruments; the children will learn a lot about the properties of sound through handling the material.
3 Make some shoebox animals that roar!

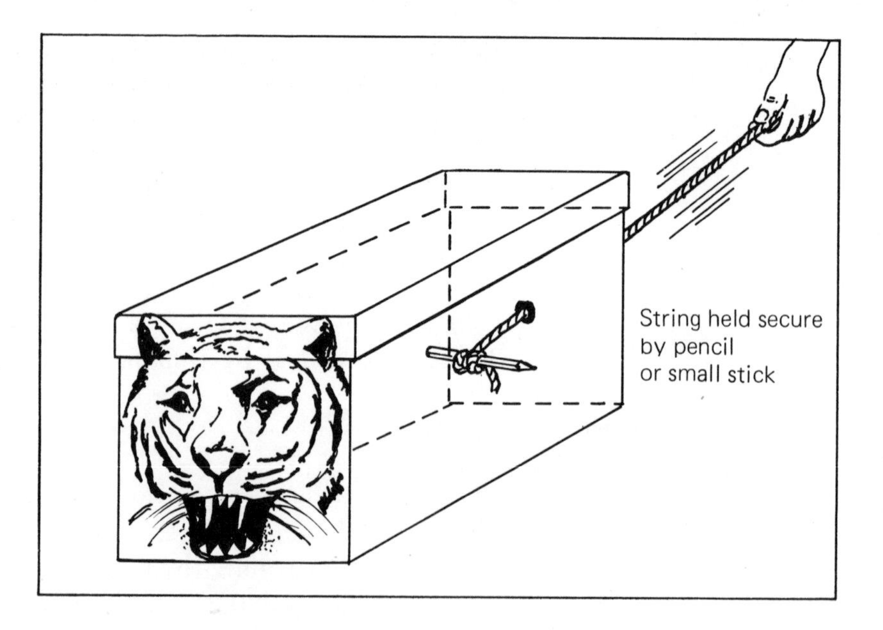

Run some chalk on the string and pull along the tail with finger and thumb. Paint a face on the front to suit the 'roar'. Try different-sized boxes and types of string.

4 Make a toy stethoscope – try listening to a watch ticking.

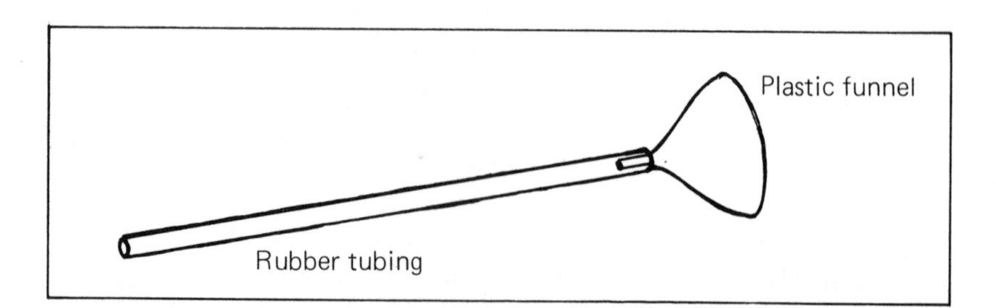

5 Try to get hold of a real stethoscope for listening to body sounds.

6 Make a megaphone out of strong card. How does it change the children's voices?

7 How else can we affect the way we hear sound?
   (a) Put hands over ears.
   (b) Put cotton wool in ears (nothing should ever be *poked* into ears).
   (c) Turn on a small transistor radio or cassette player and put it into a shoebox filled with material or a duster.

   Can the children think of any other ways of muffling sound?

8 Discuss people's voices: some are deep; some are gruff; children have high-pitched voices; some babies cry a lot. Voices are used for laughing, crying, talking, shouting, cheering; they show feeling.

9 Animals make sounds of their own: how do they use them? They have different shaped ears: how does the size of their ears help them? Try cupping hands around ears. Fish are said to make sounds that are inaudible to humans.
10 Sounds in the environment have meanings – for example those produced by the telephone, alarm clock, whistling kettle, a car's horn, an ambulance.

Ways of producing sound

When the children have had plenty of experience of making sounds by themselves, examine with them the various ways they had found of producing those sounds. They will fall roughly into these categories which are the basic groupings that can apply to musical instruments:

Percussion: *banging* – hitting, tapping, striking – virtually anything within reason

shaking – rattle, a pencil box, head of hair, wind chimes (gently)

Wind instruments: *blowing* – a whistle, kazoo, recorder, across the top of a bottle, mouth organ.

Stringed instruments: *rubbing* – hands, sand-block, hands on clothes or different materials, scrubbing brush. Drawing a violin bow across the strings is a rubbing action.

twanging – a rubber-band stretched over a box, a ruler, a guitar string.

Once through this exploratory stage, the children's natural curiosity in how things work will lead them on to try a few simple experiments.

What causes a sound?

Sound is caused by a *vibration* – a new word that will take on meaning with a few experiments.

1 The children can feel the vibration:
(a) Let them put their fingers on their throats when they speak or sing; they can also feel a cat purring.
(b) Let them feel the buzzing of tissue paper on their lips when they blow through a comb.
(c) Let them gently feel the vibrating end of a tuning fork that has just been struck, with their tongues or fingertips.
(d) Let them lightly touch a violin or guitar string that is being played, or the loudspeaker of a radio or tape recorder that is playing.

2 The children can see the vibration:
   (a) Let them sprinkle some seeds or sand onto a drumhead and watch them bounce when the drum is played.
   (b) Let them strike a tuning fork and put the vibrating end into some water or touch a suspended table-tennis ball.
   (c) Let them twang a rubber-band stretched over a box.

3 They can hear the sound!
   As you might expect, the *bigger* the vibration the *louder* the sound. The children can:
   (a) sprinkle some seeds or sand onto a drumhead and observe the change in the size of the bounce when the drum is played loudly, then very quietly;
   (b) twang a stretched rubber-band energetically, then gently, and observe the difference in the size of the movement and the sound;
   (c) do the same experiment by flipping the end of a ruler or nailfile projecting over the edge of a table;
   (d) similarly twang a guitar string;
   (e) drop a large stone, then a small stone, into a basin or pond (the water must be still) and compare the sound of the plops and the size of the ripples.

Pitch The pitch of a sound is determined by the rate of the vibration or 'frequency'; the *faster* or greater the frequency of the vibration, the *higher* the sound. Thus middle A – the note on which orchestras tune up – corresponds to a frequency of 440 vibrations per second. The lowest note on a piano has a frequency of about 25 vibrations per second and the highest note about 3,500. A *percussion sound* (drum, cymbal, shaker, etc.) doesn't seem to have a definite pitch because it is made up of a *jumble of frequencies*. (The technical way of saying so many 'vibrations per second' is so many 'cycles per second' or so many 'hertz', sometimes abbreviated to 'Hz'.)

Because the frequency of even the lowest note that can be heard (about 16 hertz) is so high, you cannot demonstrate visually the relation between pitch and rate of vibration. However you can show that when a vibrator is *shortened*, the pitch *rises* (and vice versa):

1 Pluck any guitar string: let the children hear the change in pitch as you move your finger up the string stopping each fret, and thus shortening the length of the vibrator.

2 Cover all the holes of a descant recorder, lift up the fingers one by one starting from the bottom; the children will hear the pitch rising as you blow for each note until finally all the holes are uncovered and one of the highest notes is heard.

The vibrator is the column of air inside the recorder; this is shortened as the holes are uncovered.

3 Arrange some chimebars in order of size; compare the sounds, playing from one end of the group to the other. The vibrator is the white metal part.
4 Play up and down a xylophone and a glockenspiel.
5 Blow across an empty medicine bottle; partly fill it with water and blow again. Continue until it is filled with water. The vibrator is the column of air inside (tapping gives a different result).

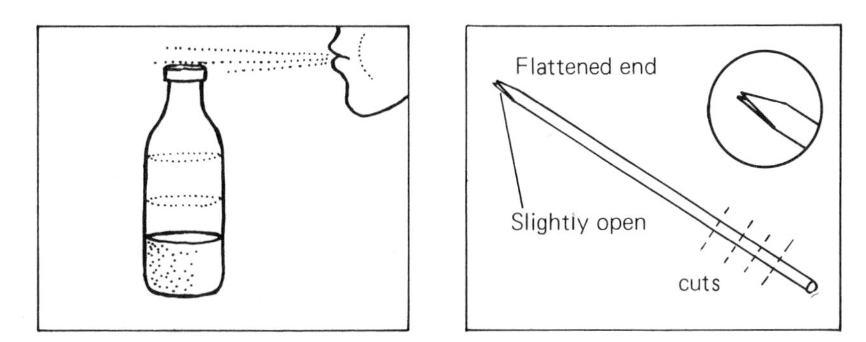

6 Show the children how to make a milk-straw pipe. Flatten and trim one end of a waxed (non-plastic) straw: blow into the cut end to get a squawk or 'raspberry'. Continue blowing but keep cutting off bits from the far end of the straw; the children will hear the pitch of the squawk rise. The vibrator is the column of air inside the straw.

The pitch of a vibrating string depends not only on its *length* but also on its *tension* and the *material from which it is made*:

1 Tighten a guitar string and listen to the pitch rise.
2 Feel the difference between the highest and lowest strings.
3 Take the front off a piano and observe the differences in the strings as you play high and low notes.

Quality The same note has a different *quality* or *character* when played on different types of instrument. This is because when a note is played on a musical instrument, higher notes are also produced which have frequencies double or treble the note played; these are called overtones or harmonics. It is the *mixture of overtones* that we hear when a single note is played that gives it its quality. Because the relative strengths of the overtones vary with the instrument, each instrument has its own distinctive quality or timbre. A tuning fork does not produce overtones, hence its 'pure' sound. A rich sound is made up of many overtones. Very high notes seem thin because the overtones are beyond our limits of hearing.

How sound travels What is actually happening when you hear a chimebar? Air is made up of millions of very small particles of gases. When tapped, the chimebar vibrates and this makes the gas particles in contact with it vibrate at the same rate. The vibrations are then transferred to other particles slightly further away from the bar and multiple collisions continue until the particles nearest to the ear press against the diaphragm, causing it to vibrate as well. A message goes up the nerves to the brain which registers that it hears a sound corresponding to that rate of vibration.

Through air *Sound travels through air* at a speed of about one mile every five seconds.

1 Observe with the children someone hammering in the distance. They will notice that they *see* each stroke before they *hear* it because light travels much faster than sound.
2 You can tell how far away a thunderstorm is by counting in seconds from the moment of the lightning flash until the first peal of thunder. Divide by five to get the distance in miles.

Through solids and liquids Sound travels through solids and liquids as well. The most obvious illustration is that sounds are continually coming into our classrooms from outside (even with the windows shut!), but here are some specific experiments:

Wood
1 Lay a ticking wristwatch down on one end of a wooden table, or desk. Listen in at the other end, with one ear touching the table.
2 Listen in while a friend taps the table with a pencil. Then listen with ears off the table and compare the sound of the taps.

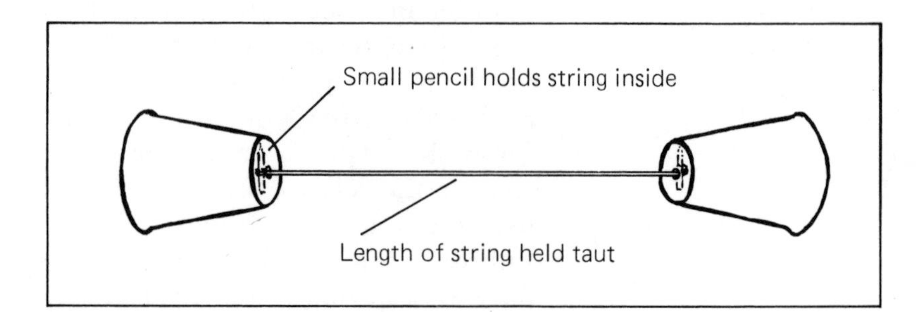

String
Show the children how to make a tin or yoghurt-carton telephone. They can try 'phoning', then speaking normally, and compare the sound of their voices. Can they hear a watch ticking through the telephone? If you've made telephones using different materials, compare results.

Metal
Tap a water pipe with a coin while a child listens, first with his ears on the pipe and then above; compare the sounds.

Ground
Bang on the playground while the children listen with their ears to the ground some way off.

Water
Bang two spoons together in a bowl of water.

Reflection of sound

Sound can be reflected from hard surfaces and the reflection is called an *echo*.

1 Can the children find any part of the school that echoes? They could also listen to sounds in places like churches or swimming baths.

2 Use two long cardboard tubes and arrange them so that a watch held at the end of one tube can be heard reflected by a wall through to the end of the other tube.

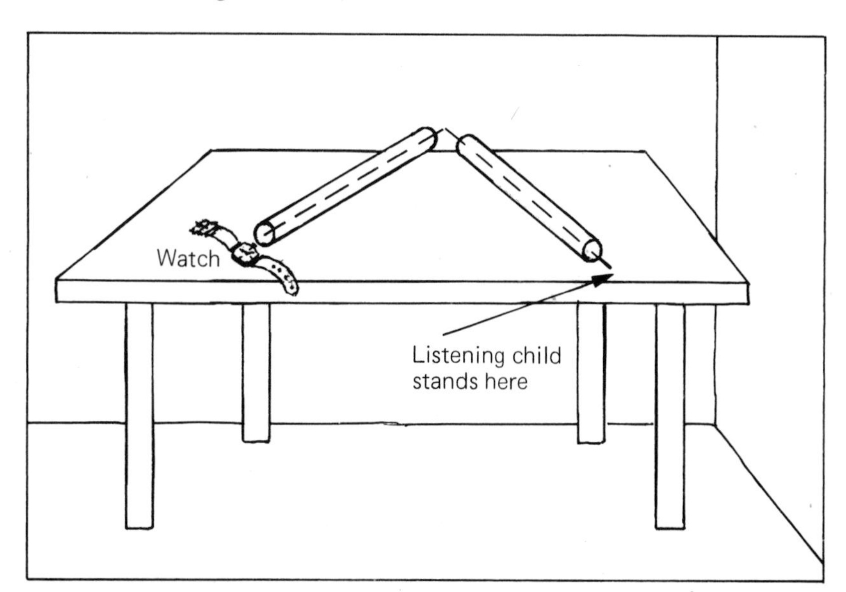

Points of interest

1. Trackers are sometimes shown listening to vibrations travelling through the ground in Wild West films.
2. Some motor mechanics use screwdrivers or similar metal objects as listening devices to help them track down odd noises.
3. Rescuers in mines listen for the bangs of trapped men.
4. Fish researchers using hydrophones (another term to explain) have reported that they can hear noises made by the fish.
5. Seamen using vibrating plates fitted to the bottom of their ships can work out how deep the sea is by sending out a note and timing the return of the echo.

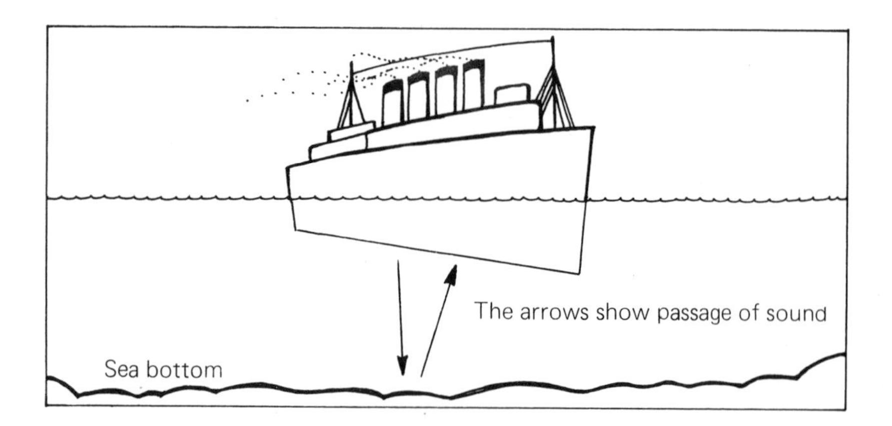

6. Can you think of any *local* illustration?

MAKING UP TUNES

Before you introduce instruments for this activity play some 'echo' games. Tell the children how sound bounces off the sides of mountains and tunnels and comes back as an echo – link your game with a story. Now 'call' some of the children's names and let the children 'echo' back. Use the pitch of the notes G–E; these sound rather like the call of the cuckoo and are commonly used by children in their chants and play songs:

	Children echo	
Susan G E		Susan G E
Anthony G G E		Anthony G G E
Where are you? G G E		Where are you? G G E

Perhaps one of the children can make up a call for you to echo. Then try longer calls with some new sounds:

Hurry up Donna. Time for tea everyone.
G A G G E G A G E E E

Now substitute an answer for the echo if you think your children are ready for this. Keep to the first two sounds to start with:

Q: What did you have for breakfast?
G G G G G G E

A: I had cornflakes.
G G G E

Using tuned instruments

When the children have had plenty of practice using these instruments freely as sound makers they will be ready to use them in a more structured way to begin making up simple tunes. I have found that chimebars are best for young children. If a xylophone or glockenspiel is used make sure that all the notes are removed except the ones you need for playing tunes.

1 Start as before with an 'echo' game using the children's names. This time accompany yourself and the children with the chimebars E and G and show the children how they can play pretend chimebars while they sing. This enables all the children to join in and gives them rhythmic practice at the same time.
2 Let the children have a turn at making a tune using their own names. Everyone echos and 'plays'.
3 Leave the chimebars in the music corner for further practice and experimentation. *Felt* beaters give a quieter sound!
4 The next time use the chimebars with snippets of conversation:

Hallo How are you?
G E G G E

Stand up everyone. Please shut the door.
G G G G E G G G E

5 Now substitute an answer for the echo if, as before, you think the children are ready. Give the chimes to one of the children for an answer and be ready to help out.
6 Leave the chimes in the music corner and encourage the children to work with a partner on similar lines – two sets of instruments would be ideal for question-and-answer tunes.
7 The range of notes for tune making can be gradually extended as the skill of the children builds up, but this should be done *very, very gradually*. Add the notes in this order – A,

D, C, C′ (or top C) making up a (pentatonic) scale on C:

C D E G A C′

These notes are within the singing range of young voices and the advantage of this scale is that tunes can begin and end on any note.

Older children who are ready to begin using the extra notes will also enjoy the challenge of making longer tunes.

1 Put together several word rhythms:

car	lorry	bicycle	van
G	A G	E E D	E

2 Use couplets, rhymes or the children's own writing.

Writing down will help the children to remember their longer tunes and enable them to play one another's. Prepare a simple sheet for the tunes:

Rain, rain G E	go away. G G	Come again a- G G A A	nother day. G G E John

Playing together can sustain interest and give pleasure to more able children.

1 Add a drone – a repeated low note played on the strong beat.
2 Add an ostinato:

	Rain, rain	go away.	Come again a-	nother day.
Tune	G E	G G E	G G A A	G G E
Drone	C	C	C	C
Ostinato	GA GA	G A G A	G A G A	G A G A

3 Try different arrangements:
Play the tune – add the drone.
Play the tune – add the ostinato.
Play the tune – add the drone first time;
add the ostinato as well the second time.
Vary the ways of playing – loudly, quietly, quickly, slowly.
Add a group of children to sing the tune.

Any combination of these variations will enable you to involve the children in group music making based on simple material which can be extended according to the developing skills of the children. Use longer rhymes and add simple percussion instruments.

Further reading

Several suggestions for class **sound pictures** are given in the Teacher's Books 1 and 2 of *Topic Anthologies* by Jean Gilbert (Oxford University Press, 1980), while Mary Pape describes a school project 'Noah's Journey' in her book *Growing Up with Music* (Oxford University Press, 1970).

Some good pictorial talking points about **sound** are contained in the Ladybird Leader *Sounds* (Ladybird Books, 1975). See also the chapter 'Listening to things' in *Early Experiences: Beginnings* (Macdonald Educational, 1972). John Hosier's book *Instruments of the Orchestra* (Oxford University Press, 1961) contains an excellent section 'About Sound'. Ways of producing sound are explored further in *Musical Instruments* (Ladybird Books, 1970) and Section 2 of *Teaching Primary Science: Musical Instruments* (Macdonald Educational, 1976); the latter also outlines experiments suitable for infants and lower juniors.

5 THE MUSIC CORNER

Incorporating musical activities into the daily classroom programme adds breadth to many other areas of the curriculum and the provision of a music corner will enable every child to participate at his own level and at his own pace. However if these activities are to be worth while, enjoyable and survive their initial introduction, they must be planned to fit in with each particular classroom's organization. It would be so much easier if we all had purpose-built sound-proofed areas!

WHERE TO SITE THE MUSIC CORNER

Some schools have a central area like a hall, or a small room or annexe; others use shared corridors, which is more suitable for older children. The disadvantage in both cases is that the teacher cannot hear what is going on unless she frequently leaves the classroom. One solution is to have a trolley timetabled for use in the classroom at specific times. Teachers in spread-out or open-plan schools will probably need to co-operate in setting up their corners. Wherever the instruments are, there should be adequate supervision of their use and control of their safety.

With younger children the best place is in or very near to their own classroom or working area. The siting of the corner is very much a personal choice and determined to some extent by the physical structure of the building. It needs to be as far away as possible from the most common areas of movement and it is a good idea to have some form of screening to encourage concentration and protect the class from some of the sound. Curtaining, pegboard or the back of bookcases could be used, or even one of those carrels with built-in absorbent surfaces normally available for audio-visual equipment, if the height is right.

Some helpful advice

1. Limit the number of children who can use the corner at any one time.
2. Withdraw the use of the corner at certain times of the day if you feel the activity is likely to disrupt the rest of the class.
3. Encourage quiet activity if noise level worries you. Provide sound makers like small shakers, little bells and sand-blocks.

4 Start with a modest corner and only very gradually extend the scope.
5 Try to plan so that the activities arise out of what you have been doing with the children. Give them specific assignments to do and take an interest in what is going on; this can be difficult when there is so much else to do but it *does* pay dividends.
6 Do use good visual stimuli – pictures, paintings, books, children's stories, workcards, etc.
7 Remember that very young children need plenty of time to *repeat* their activities. Older children should have slightly more direction, such as workcards, built into their activities.
8 Encourage the children to *remember* what they have done or discovered. Playing back a little tune or rhythm is not only good for them but encourages the others.
9 It is a good idea to resite the area occasionally to give the children and yourself fresh stimulus, and sometimes everyone benefits if it is withdrawn completely for one or two longer periods.

MUSIC-CORNER CHECKLIST

Essential equipment

Try to build up a good *variety* of instruments:

shakers, tambourines, clappers, bells, wood-blocks, triangles (home-made instruments are ideal – see Chapter 6).

Have a set of chimebars – C, D, E, F, G, A, B, C′, D′, E′ – plus F♯ and B♭ if possible, and different kinds of beaters – rubber, wooden, felt.

Collect a box of 'bits and pieces' – objects made of wood, metal, plastic, card, etc.

Useful extras

For a more sophisticated (adequately supervised) area:

xylophone (preferably alto), glockenspiel (preferably alto), metallophone, large maracas, reso-reso scraper or guiro (rasp), claves, bongos, large suspended cymbal – use a padded beater, good tambour, two-tone woodblock, good drum with suitable beaters.

The music corner can reflect other areas of the curriculum and will probably house from time to time things like shells, water chimes, puppets, sorting trays and so on.

SOUND EXPERIMENTS AND GAMES

Here are just a few ways of structuring the activities in the music corner; many more will arise out of the activities you plan for the children.

1 Sound pairing; six or eight identical non-transparent shakers; *two of each* have the *same contents*. Use the same idea with chimebars/glockenspiel/xylophone.

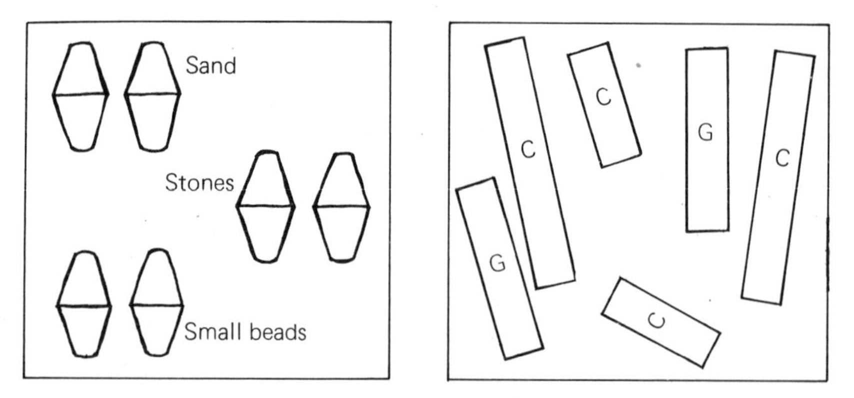

2 *Sound guessing*: Put *different* fillings into several identical *transparent* containers and completely cover one half of each container. Working with a partner, the children try to guess what the filling is.

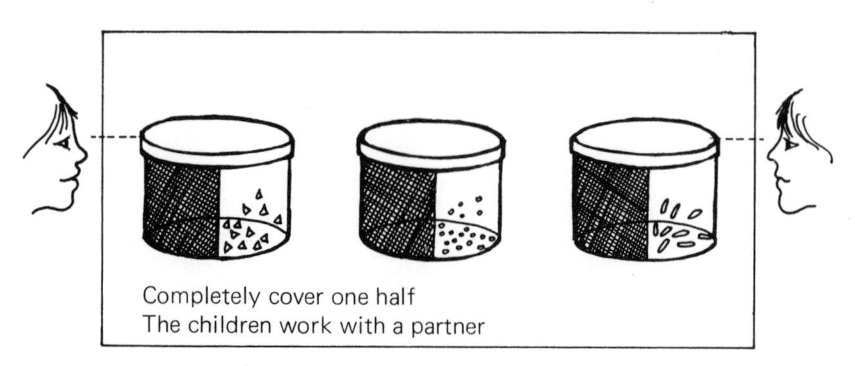
Completely cover one half
The children work with a partner

3 *Sound sorting*: Make cards which sort sounds into sets (use one set to begin with):

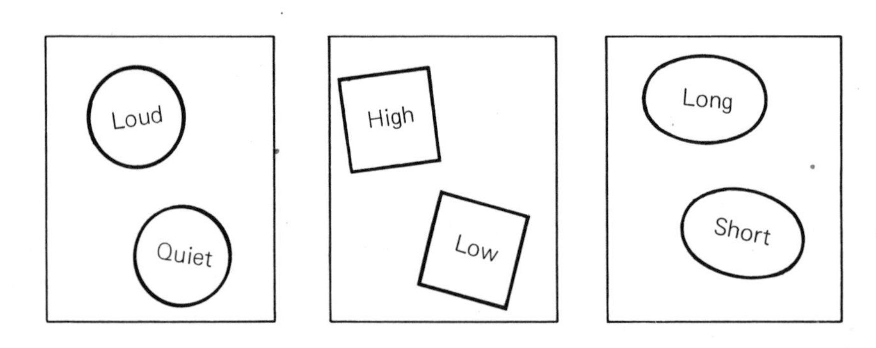

Encourage the children to listen to sounds that they can hear outside their houses at night. Swop experiences the next day; get the children to match up the remembered sounds on instruments or other sound makers. Make a recording yourself one night and ask the children to identify the sounds.

Hiawatha's Boyhood
At the door on summer evenings
Sat the little Hiawatha;
Heard the whispering of the pine trees,
Heard the lapping of the water. . . .

An evocative night picture is contained in this part of the *Hiawatha* ballad.

'Things that go "bump" in the night' by Spike Milligan[23]

Song
'Night Piece'[22]

Listening
Nocturnes by Chopin (calm)
Night on the Bare Mountain by Mussorgsky (exciting)

Butterflies **Sound poems**

Butterflies
All day long in the garden
Are butterflies flitting by,
White, pale yellow, and orange bright
And some like the blue of the sky.
Clive Sansom

Sound picture
The children can imitate the flight of the butterfly on suitable instruments. Then let them choose different instruments for the four colours and play in four groups, the sounds in each group coming and going, stopping and starting, playing slowly, quickly, loudly, quietly. They must listen carefully to vary the playing of their own instrument within their own group. Organize this yourself to start with, then let one of the children do the conducting.

Hallowe'en **Sound picture** suggesting an event and possibly linked with a story, e.g. 'The Once-a Year Witch' by J. Varga (Pergamon Press, 1974).

A witch's kitchen	*Suggested sound makers*
Wind	voices – *oo-oos* sung at different pitches – going up and down – getting loud, then quiet again
Cauldron crackling	shakers; crumpled newspaper
Witch laughing	voice
Spell	a slide on the xylophone followed by a few notes on the chimes or glock
Frog	clappers, sticks or wood-block
Spider	gentle slides on guiro, rasp or wooden washboard

The chart below suggests one arrangement, but virtually any combination and order of sounds will make an interesting composition. Try several; tape them and discuss the results.

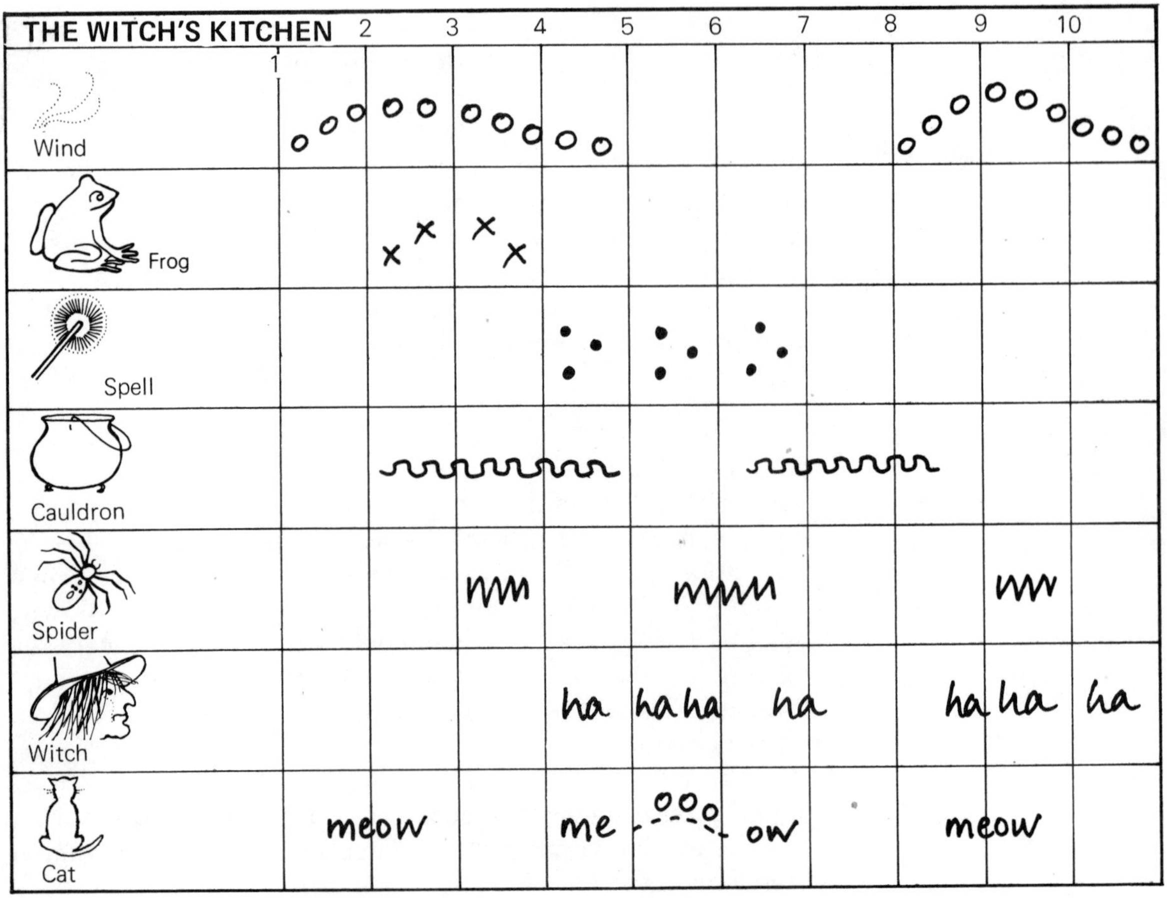

THE WITCH'S KITCHEN	1	2	3	4	5	6	7	8	9	10
Wind	o o o	o o	o o o	o o				o o	o o o	o o o
Frog		x x	x x							
Spell				• • •	• • •	• • •				
Cauldron		~~~	~~~	~~~		~~~	~~~	~~~		
Spider			ʌʌʌ		ʌʌʌ	ʌʌʌ			ʌʌʌ	
Witch				ha	ha ha	ha			ha ha	ha
Cat	meow			me	ooo	ow			meow	

Poems

Heigh ho! for Hallowe'en.
All the witches to be seen,
Some black and some green,
Heigh ho! for Hallowe'en.
(Anon)

There was an old witch,
Believe it if you can,
She tapped on the window,
And she ran, ran, ran.
She ran helter-skelter,
With her toes in the air,
Cornstalks flying
From the old witch's hair.

'Swish' goes the broomstick,
'Meow' goes the cat,
'Plop' goes the hop toad
Sitting on her hat.
'Wee' chuckled I,
'What fun, fun, fun!'
Hallowe'en night
When the witches run.
(Words traditional)

Hallowe'en[24] by Leonard Clark
Shadows and Spells[25]
'Witch Witch' by Rose Fyleman[23]
'The Ride by Nights' by Walter de la Mare[26]
'The Witches' Chant' by William Shakespeare[26]

Songs

Weather Witch[20]
Hallowe'en[27]
Hallowe'en is coming[5]
Witch Song[5]
There was an old witch[1]
Skin and Bones[6]
Witches of Hallowe'en[28]
Hallowe'en Coming[7]

Stories

The Once-a-Year Witch
Meg and Mog[6]
The Good Bad Witch[28]

Listening

'In the Hall of the Mountain King' from *Peer Gynt* Suite by Grieg

Hänsel and Gretel by Humperdinck

The Wind

Sound picture

Choose a windy day to focus on local gusty sounds; encourage the children to think of phrases to describe what they have seen, felt or heard on a windy day. Assemble some ideas and shape them into a class tone poem. Write it down and get the children to accompany their poem with suitable sounds.

Poems

The following is a good poem to inspire creative writing on this theme, or use it as a sound poem with younger children.

Wind Song	*Suggested percussion*
When the wind blows	
The quiet things speak.	whispering
Some whisper, some clang,	a clapper
Some creak.	quiet 'rasp'
Grasses swish.	voices
Treetops sigh.	voices
Flaps slap	a clap
and snap at the sky.	clappers
Wires on poles	
whistle and hum	voices
Ashcans roll.	tambourine
Windows drum.	drum

When the wind goes –
suddenly
then,
the quiet things
are quiet again.
Lilian Moore

'Windy Nights' by Robert Louis Stevenson[29]
'When the wind is in the east'[30]
'The Wind' by James Reeves[31]

Alternatively this poem invites a more rhythmic accompaniment:

Windy Nights	*Suggested accompaniment*
Rumbling in the chimneys,	drum
Rattling at the doors	tambourine
Round the roofs and round the roads	low chimebar
The rude wind roars;	
Raging through the darkness,	drum
Raving through the trees,	tambourine
Racing off again across	drum and tambourine
The great grey seas	gradually getting quieter
Rodney Bennett	

Create your own sound picture of the wind, using ideas from these and other poems and from the children.

	Suggested sound makers
Wind	voices (ooo—)
Telephone wires humming	voices (mmm—)
Trees blowing	shakers
Gate banging	clappers
Dustbin lid rolling along	cymbal (or saucepan and spoon – even a dustbin lid)
Paper-bags being blown along	paper (tissue, newspaper, etc.)
Washing flapping on the line	flap a small piece of material or sheet of newspaper

Suggested arrangement

The sound of the wind and telephone wires humming can be in the background all the time. They can suddenly increase to represent a gust of wind and the 'gust' can be followed by one or two of the suggested sounds. The wind can die down at the end. Thus the pattern would be:

Wind and telephone wires sound – a gust of wind is followed by a gate banging and a line of washing flapping. The wind dies down, then a further gust is followed by a dustbin lid clanking along, etc. Finish with the voices of the wind and the wires gradually getting quieter and quieter until they stop altogether.

Using a visual 'score' (see below) is another way of conducting a sound picture. When the children are ready to play, move your finger, or a pointer very slowly *from left to right*. The children play when the pointer reaches their bit and stop when it moves on. You can move your finger back if you want to extend or continue a part; you can play right through several times in different ways – going quickly/slowly, playing loudly/quietly, etc.

Songs
The wind blows east[5]
Falling leaves[6]
The north wind doth blow[6]
Windy old weather[32]
The mill wheel[20]
Weather witch[20]

Finger play
Five little leaves[5]

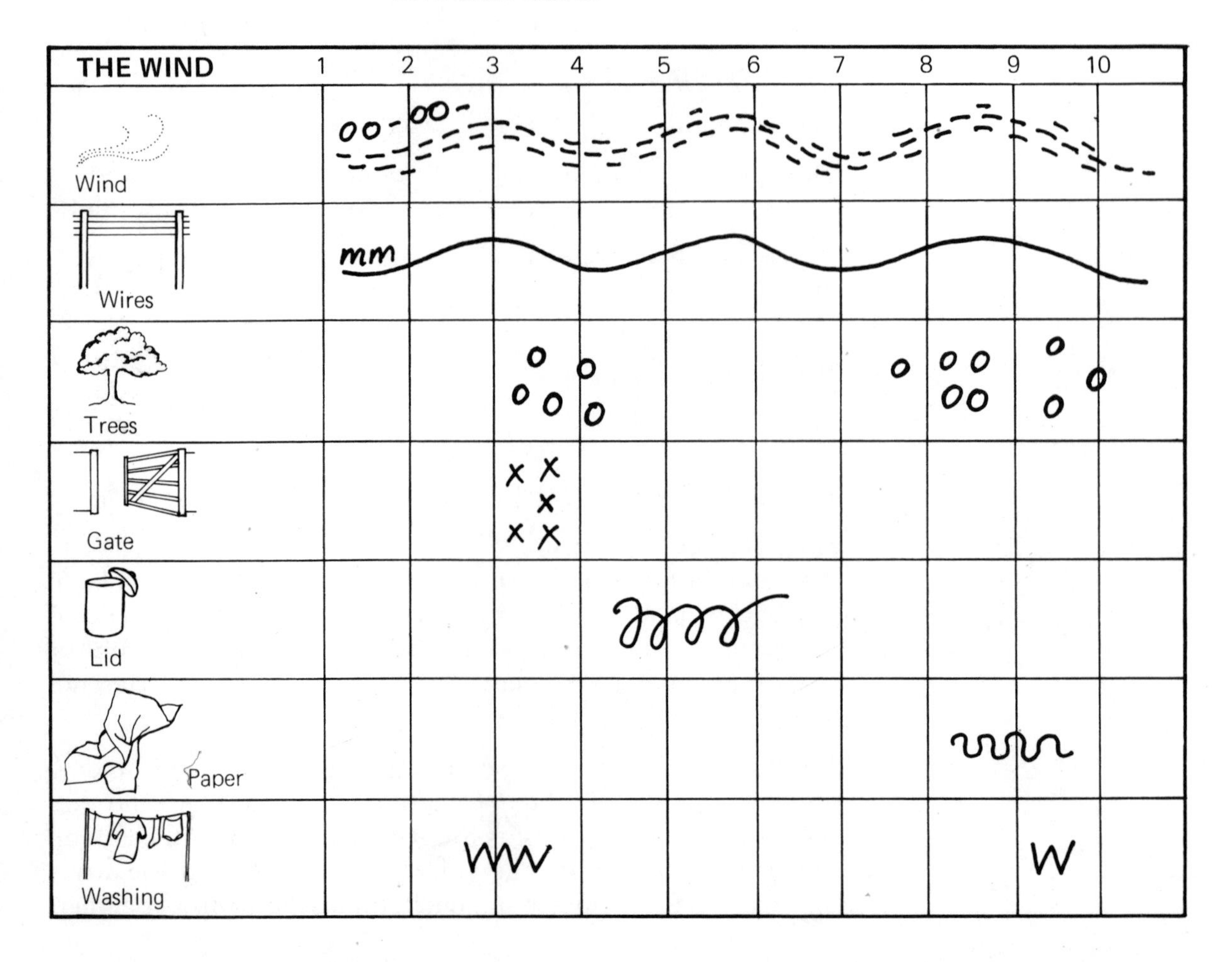

Noah's Ark

Sound sequence

The story of the Ark is a rich source of ideas for work in exploring sound and dramatic movement. It is a long narrative and with older children it is best to divide it into parts so that musical interest can be sustained through the more detailed ideas that can be encouraged this way.

Story line	*Suggested sound makers*
Part 1: Noah and his family build the ark.	
Chopping trees	clappers or wood banged with a stick
Sawing wood	a guiro, wooden washboard or corrugated card. Try different sticks for the 'saw'.
Hammering (small)	clappers (or claves)
(big)	drum or tambour
Sandpapering	sandpaper blocks
Painting	soft brush on drum or tambour head
People talking	children whispering in a group making up 'mini' conversations; occasionally a laugh directed at Noah

Part 2: The animals arrive. (This should be preceded by talking about the way different animals move and linking with movement; it could form the basis for several hall sessions. The sounds could be played one after another in a kind of procession, or there could be a build up as more and more animals approach the ark.)

Snakes, worms – 'crawlies' in general	sandpaper blocks; rustled or crumpled paper of differing textures – insides of chocolate boxes etc.
Birds, butterflies and flying creatures	bells, jingles, random notes on the glockenspiel or chimebars
Rabbits, kangaroos and creatures that hop	clappers; beats on a tambour or drum in a 'hopping' rhythm
Elephants and big lumbering animals	a drum or bass xylophone if you have one (try the effects of different beaters)

Horses, ponies, donkeys, zebras and trotting animals	coconuts – several pairs preferably, going at different speeds

(The list is endless, but it is best to agree upon specific groups and aim for a variety of sound within each group.)

The main door closes when the Ark is full.	drum

Part 3: The rain comes.

Light rain	xylophone, tapped triangle
Heavy rain	shakers, bells
Thunder	a roll on a big drum or several rubber drums are effective played with chimebar beaters
Lightning	a cymbal – use a padded beater

It is difficult to get the effect of rain *gradually* becoming faster and heavier, so allow the children time to practise. Encourage them to *listen* carefully to one another.

The rain gradually eases off.	rain sounds quieten gradually; finish with the triangle
The raven and the dove are sent out of the ark	bells; xylophone

Part 4: Noah, his family and all the animals come out of the ark.

	Repeat the animal music from Part 2 and add a 'whispering' group to represent the humans.
The rainbow	a peal of slow notes on 'glockenspiel', chimebars or, best of all, metallophone

Poems

The Young Puffin Book of Verse (Penguin 1970) has a section on 'All the animals'.

Songs

The animals went in two by two[1]
Who built the Ark[33]
One more river[34]

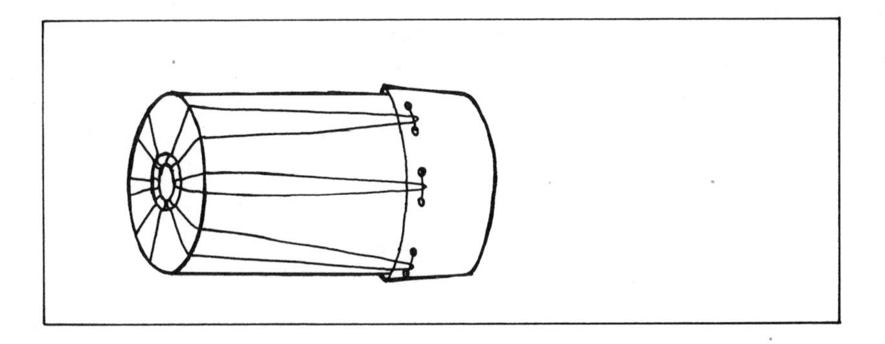

Drumsticks Make a hole in a solid hardwood ball and glue in a piece of dowel rod.

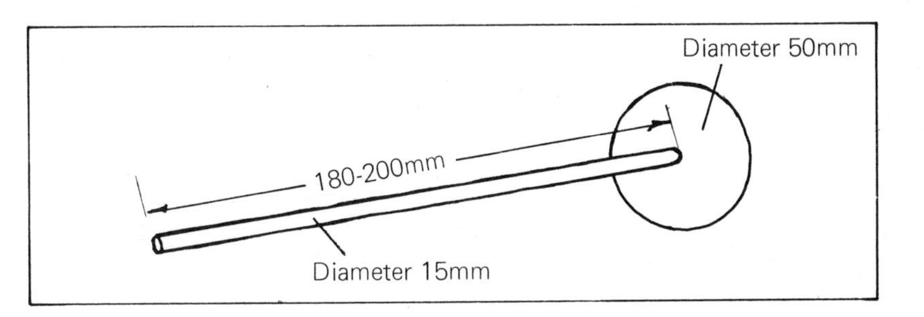

Clappers *Materials*
Two pieces of flat wood or the base and lid of a wooden date-box and two cotton-reels.
Method
Sandpaper the wood and screw or stick the cotton-reels onto the centre. Paint (two coats are best) and finish with two coats of a good clear varnish; this preserves the paint and improves the sound of the 'click'.

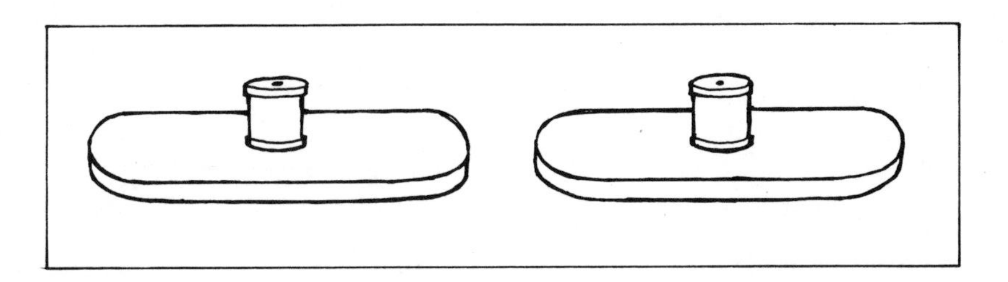

Coconuts Smooth away the outside of a small coconut and get a friend to help you saw it in half. Scrape out the flesh; sandpaper all over. Bore a hole in the centre of each half and improvise handles from drawer-knobs or leather strips. Walnut shell halves make baby clip-clops!

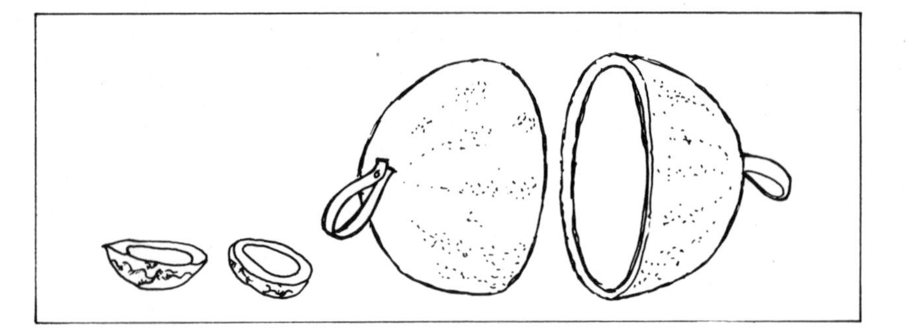

Rhythm sticks

Material
Dowelling – 5 mm or 15 mm thick cut into suitable lengths – 150 mm or 200 mm.
Method
Sandpaper all over; paint and varnish.

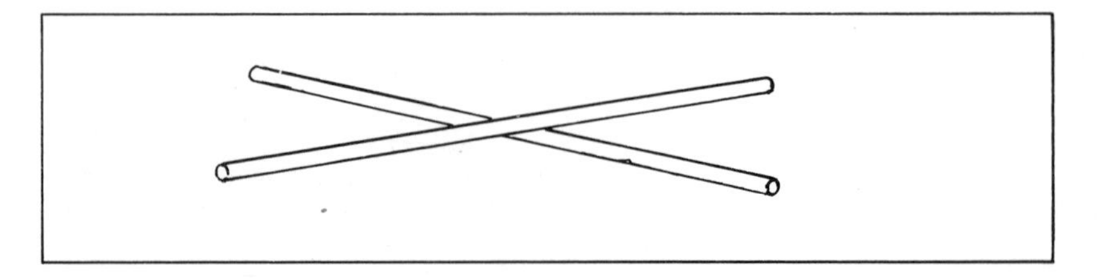

Bells

Materials
Metal bottle-tops, firm wire (coat hanger), a smooth piece of wood or dowelling for a handle.
Method
Remove the plastic lining of the bottle-tops if you can (this gives a better sound) and make a hole in the centre by hammering a nail through onto a piece of old wood. Thread the bottle-tops, back to back, onto the wire and secure each end into the wooden handle. Paint and varnish the handle.

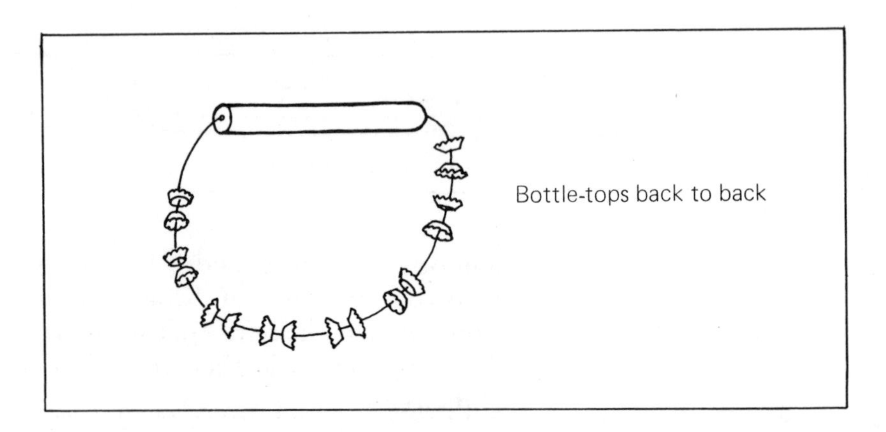

Jingles As for bells, but thread two bottle-tops back to back onto each nail which is driven into a smooth piece of wood. Paint and varnish the wooden holder.

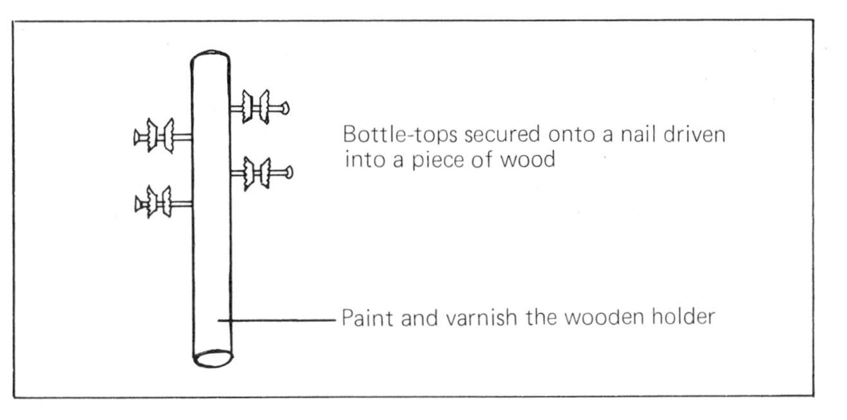

Tambourines *Materials*
4 picnic plates, metal bottle-tops, open curtain rings.
Method
Glue all the plates together. Paint and varnish. Punch holes around the edge. Thread two bottle-tops, back to back, onto an open curtain ring and fasten through the holes, or alternate with ribbons.

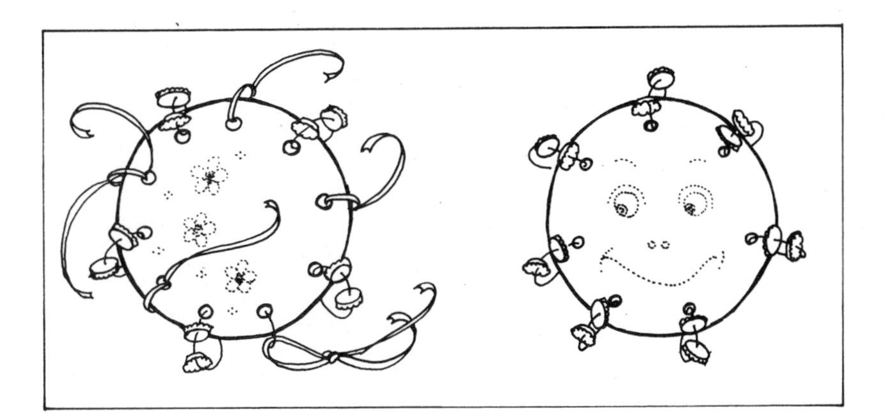

Scrapers Saw notches across a piece of bamboo and use a rhythm stick for scraping. Reeded hardboard or a wooden washboard also make good scrapers.

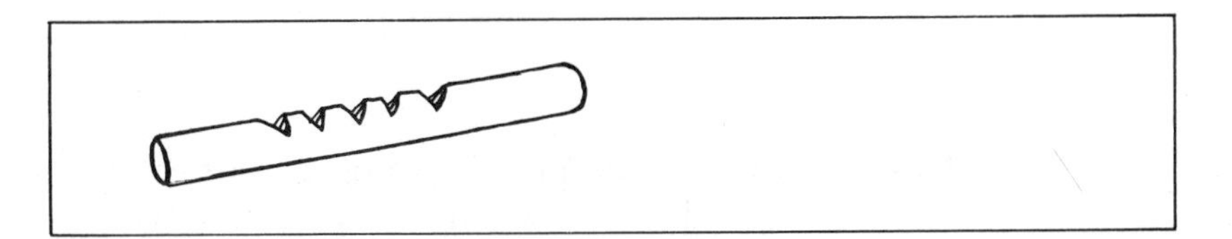

Sand-blocks Cover the ends of two blocks of wood of handling size with sandpaper, using glue or drawing pins. Improvise handles if necessary.

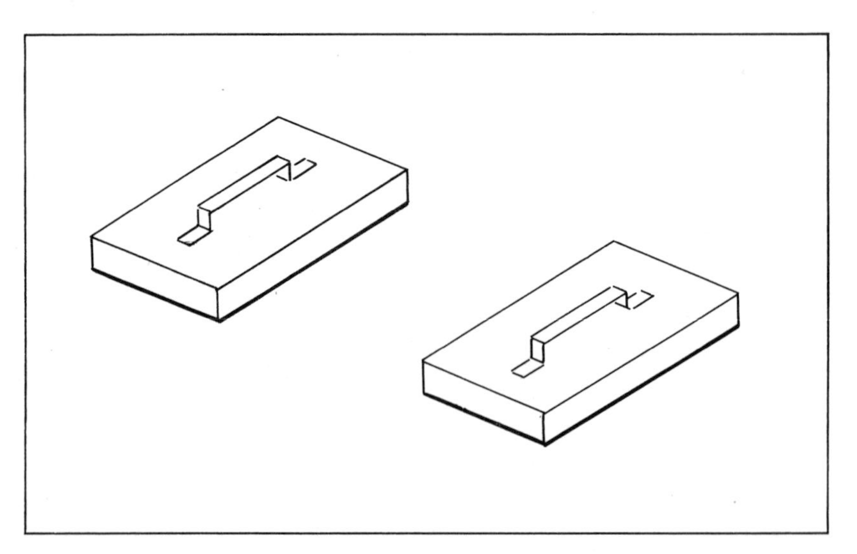

Shakers *Materials*

Tins, boxes, plastic bottles or conrtainers, yoghurt cartons, etc. Various fillings – sand, salt, beans, rice, sago, buttons, pebbles, nails, etc.

Method

It is important to vary the shape, material, size and sound. Leave some transparent containers uncovered for identification of contents; otherwise decorate or cover with *Contact*. Make sure the lids are secured with a strong glue.

Maraca-type shakers can be made from plastic lemon-type containers. Improvise handles from thin rods or newspaper; paint and varnish.

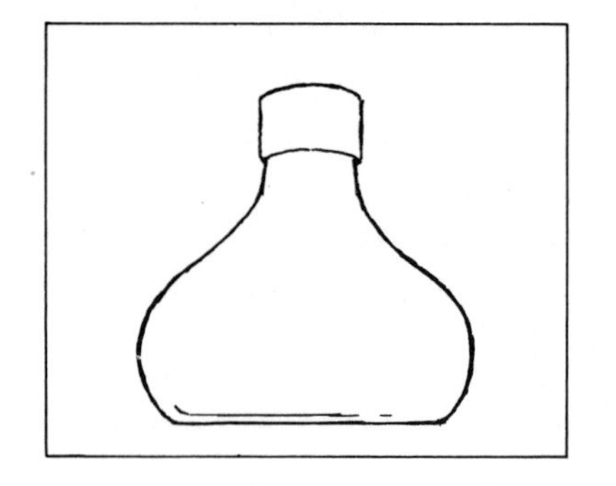

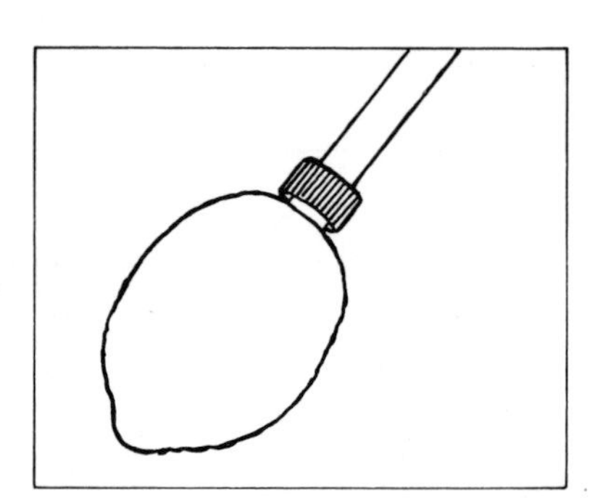

Tone-blocks Use empty cigar boxes. Cut shapes out of the lid or sides, then glue or nail the lid on. Strike with a rhythm stick or drumstick.

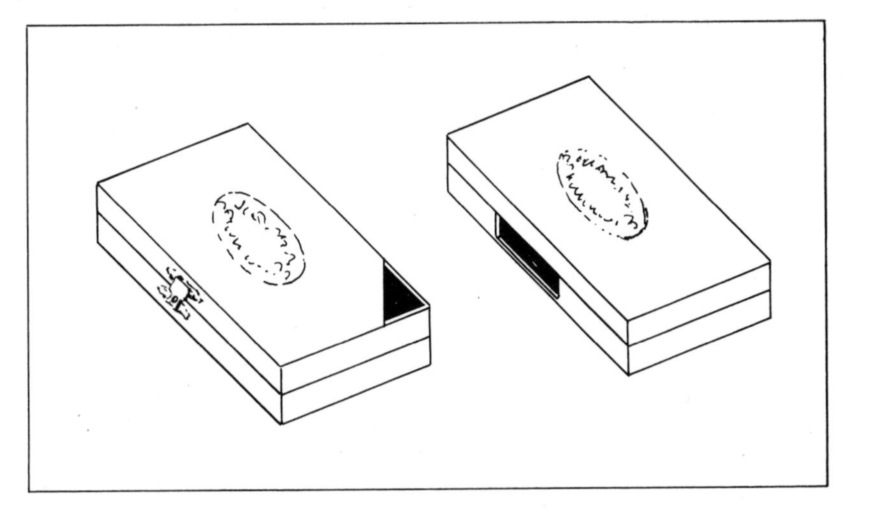

Percussion-group instruments

Sets of instruments will have to be sturdy to withstand frequent use in percussion groups and many of them, like the drums, cannot be tackled successfully by younger children. This is a time-consuming job for one teacher, but sometimes teachers in local junior or secondary schools are willing to make instruments as part of their craft work; parents and older brothers and sisters are often willing to help as well. Sometimes a course can be organized through the local teachers' centre.

Once a sufficient number of instruments has been acquired, they can be kept in the classroom for use with percussion groups, and a well-made set will last for years.

7 AUDIO-VISUAL AIDS FOR THE TEACHER

Radio and television broadcasts, as well as recorded music, are valuable sources for teaching ideas in the classroom. A skilled teacher can use them to provide music for movement, for songs and games, and as a means of encouraging the children to listen.

Although we would all agree that young children should experience musical sound at first hand, few of us can provide in school an adequate range of live musical performances. Most children are exposed to music at home through the radio, television and records, and if we decide to use any of these media in the classroom, it is important to encourage good attitudes and listening habits that will also benefit the young home listener.

RADIO AND TELEVISION

There are many suitable programmes on both radio and television: some provide a direct link with music – such as the *Music and Movement* series on radio, *Music Box, Time and Tune* and *Music Time* on television; others use music as an integral part of an overall programme, like *Sounds, Words and Music* and *Listen with Mother* on radio, and *Talkabout* and *Seeing and Doing* on television. There will be other suitable programmes on local radio stations and a wealth of music – from pop to classical – broadcast throughout the day that can be used for clapping, dancing, moving and listening.

The important thing is to find out well in advance what is available and the teachers' notes which accompany many programmes (several months' advance ordering is usually required) will give a clear idea of a programme's suitability. The *Radio Times* has a day-by-day coverage. Termly forecasts can be obtained from The School Broadcasting Council for the United Kingdom (30/LND), The Langham, Portland Place, London W1M 4AA, and ITV Publications Ltd (Schools Department), 247 Tottenham Court Road, London W1P 0AU.

Radio programmes are best taped, for many reasons: the teacher can listen to the programme beforehand, decide if it is suitable and prepare the children. (Programmes which are not suitable for listening all the way through may still provide ideas for the teacher to use.) Taping also means that the programme can be used at the *right time* for the children; it can be heard again another day if necessary, and is available to other classes. Then there is the obvious advantage of being able to stop and start the tape so that bits of the programme can be explained or heard again. Label the tape clearly for quick identification and store centrally.

The BBC pamphlet *School Broadcasting: A Guide for Teachers* gives good advice on the taping of broadcasts and how to use programmes more effectively with classes. These recordings may be retained for three years under the conditions given in the Annual Programme 'Recording Concessions'. The Annual Programme also gives information on obtaining good Radio 4 VHF reception under the following headings: 'Radio reception' and 'Quality of sound: radio in the classroom'.

RECORDED MUSIC

There is much valuable recorded material in the form of songs, singing games, listening music, music to move to and illustrated stories. Some suggestions are given in Appendix 2. Visit the local record shop and, if there is one, browse in the record department of the public library. Ask the children if they have any favourite records their parents would allow them to bring to school (take great care of them!).

The tape recorder

It is much easier to use a tape recorder than a turntable when working with young children, especially if only a small snippet of music is needed, or several small snippets for movement. The answer is to pre-record on tape (read through the notes at the end of this chapter), and this you can now do if your school owns the record and if your Authority has taken out a licence with the Mechanical Copyright Protection Society Ltd.

It is a good idea to make your own collection of short musical excerpts on tape for permanent use with your classes, for example:

light 'Dance of the Mirlitons' (or Reed-Pipes) from the *Nutcracker Suite* by Tchaikovsky
march March from *The Love of Three Oranges* by Prokofiev
dramatic 'In the Hall of the Mountain King' from *Peer Gynt* by Grieg
gay Peter's tune from *Peter and the Wolf* by Prokofiev
quiet/lyrical 'The Swan' from *Carnival of the Animals* by Saint-Saëns.

Label the tape in sufficient detail and keep it accessible. This kind of tape can be used in many ways – 'The Swan' when some 'settling' music is needed, or a march to go with a soldier song. Use it too for clapping, movement and specific listening.

One of the most useful tapes I have ever made consisted of a few simple tunes that the children knew, and programmed so that each piece contrasted in some way with the next one and was preceded by a short thinking signal:

(piano) The Grand Old Duke of York *march*
(piano) Boys and girls come out to play *skipping*
(xylophone) Yankee Doodle *running*
(glockenspiel) Twinkle, twinkle, little star *quietly*
(piano) London Bridge is falling down *heavy*
(glockenspiel) As I lay on the golden sands *light, swaying*
(piano) Baa, baa, black sheep *steady; march*

This was ideal for use in the classroom with beginner percussion groups (see Chapter 3); it was good too for clapping, singing, moving and listening. Similar tapes, based on the children's favourite songs, can be made. If you do not play an instrument, enlist the help of a musical friend or parent or even a music teacher from a neighbouring school. It takes time, good judgment and care to make tapes, but the effort is well worth while. Once made, the tapes are always available and can be added to at any time. Remember to label each tape clearly and keep it handy.

Here are some more ideas:

1 Make a puzzle tape of everyday sounds – tap running, footsteps, dog barking, baby crying, aeroplane overhead, door shutting, kettle whistling . . . (see also Chapter 1).
2 Make up a puzzle tape of radio and TV jingles and current programme music.
3 Record some of the children's favourite songs: sing them yourself or enlist the help of some of the older juniors or brothers or sisters. The tape can be used in a quiet listening corner, preferably with the use of headphones.
4 Let the children suggest sounds to record and to play back to another group as a quiz.
5 Let the children try recording their own little stories with sound effects.
6 Organize a cassette swop when each class or group records a few favourite songs. Children love being recorded and will always listen intently (and critically) to their own performance and to that of their friends.

Choosing a tape recorder

There are four types of machine: reel-to-reel recorder; cassette recorder; cassette player; combined radio and cassette recorder:

Reel-to-reel recorder A reel (spool) of tape is placed on one spindle, the tape is threaded through a central mechanism to an empty reel on a second spindle.

Advantages
The sound quality can be very good, most of the machines give sufficient volume, and the tape can be edited.

Disadvantages
Threading the tape can be rather fiddly, and the machines tend to be big and heavy.

Cassette recorder Simply snap in a cassette and switch on.

Advantages
Machines are very easy to operate, light in weight and can be quite cheap.

Disadvantages
Unless you pay a lot of money, the sound quality and volume are not up to reel-to-reel standards; editing is difficult. Some cassette recorders work on batteries, but these run down fairly quickly and it is probably cheaper in the long run to buy a battery/mains machine.

Cassette player This plays cassettes that have already been made on a cassette recorder.

Advantages
Cheap, portable, easily operated even by a young child, and tapes cannot be erased by mistake. If you can afford to do so, buy a cassette recorder which you keep at home to make your recordings, and one or two players for use with, or by, the children.

Combined radio and cassette recorder With this, recording a radio broadcast simply involves pressing a couple of buttons.

For advice on the actual model to meet your needs, consult the audio-visual adviser if your education authority has one. In Scotland a free advisory service is available from the Scottish Centre for Educational Technology, 74, Victoria Crescent Road, Dowanhill, Glasgow G12 9JN.

Maintenance All machines need regular maintenance. It is especially important to clean the 'head' periodically. This isn't difficult if the instruction book's guidelines are followed.

Headphones and junction boxes Using headphones enables children to listen to cassette recordings in the classroom without being distracted by the rest of the class and without in turn distracting them. Groups of up to six can listen together by means of a junction box connected to the recorder.

MAKING RECORDINGS

Using a microphone

It is best to use the microphone supplied with the machine. Read the instruction book carefully, especially with regard to the recording level. If the recorder has a manual/automatic level switch, better results will be obtained on the manual setting as long as the instructions are carefully followed. Experiment with the distance between the microphone and the source of the recording in order to get crisp quality and to minimize echoes. Remember that the quality can be affected by the size and furnishing of a room and, if possible, try different rooms. Don't embark on a long and difficult recording without first making a short trial and checking the result. Attention to these details will result in surprisingly good recordings from even the cheapest equipment.

From record player or radio

If the microphone is placed directly in front of the loudspeaker the result will be poor. Most record players and radios have an output socket which can be connected by a special lead to the tape recorder and this is the way to get really good quality. The audio-visual adviser can probably help here; otherwise, consult a local dealer. With a little care, a recording can be made that sounds almost as good as the original.

Getting advice

If there is a local audio-visual adviser, he will be glad to help. Otherwise it is quite likely that a parent of one of the children is something of a technical expert, and can show you what to do; the local radio dealer will probably be helpful if the situation is explained. Modern equipment can be so good that there is really no excuse for subjecting children to poor-quality sound.

Copyright

The BBC has made a special arrangement that permits the copying of school broadcasts. Gramophone records can be copied if the local Authority has taken out a licence with the Mechanical Copyright Protection Society Ltd. Ask the head-teacher for further details.

APPENDIX I MUSIC METHODS: SOME WELL-KNOWN APPROACHES

There are a number of specific methods of teaching music in schools.

Curwen Method

John Curwen (1816–80) was a gifted teacher of young children and pioneer of reforms inspired by Pestalozzi. He was musically self-taught and it was from his own experiences, both as a teacher and a learner, that he formulated a method of teaching children to sing, known as *Tonic Sol-fa*. His principles and methods have been revived and brought up to date: they include the use of the sol-fa syllables to train the ear to pitch notes relative to one another; the use of hand signs while singing, and the deliberate development of musical memory.

The New Curwen Method Book 1 is available from The Curwen Institute, 108 High Street, London SW11 3HP.

Kodály Method

Originating in Hungary, this uses the medium of singing and singing games to train the ear and to approach musical concepts and musical literacy. It employs the use of sol-fa (singing games – do, re, mi, fa, so, la, ti, do), hand signs for the introduction of pitch and time names for rhythm training.

The Kodály Way to Music by Cecilia Vajda (Boosey & Hawkes, 1974) explains the method adapted for British schools. Other titles include *The Kodály Method* by Lois Choksy (Prentice-Hall, 1974), a comprehensive music education from Infant to Adult; *The Kodály Concept of Music Education* by Helga Szabo (English edition by Geoffrey Russell-Smith) accompanied by three LPs (SBHED 0003) (Boosey & Hawkes, 1969); *Let's Sing Together* by Denise Bacon (Boosey & Hawkes, 1971), songs for the threes, fours and fives.

Dalcroze Eurythmics

This was developed by Emile Jaques-Dalcroze (1865–1950), a Swiss musician. His method teaches musical rhythms, shapes and structures through bodily movements; it is usually a group activity and lends itself to many teaching techniques. The main characteristics are:

1 the vital enjoyment of rhythmic movement and the confidence it gives;

2 the ability to hear, understand and express music through movement;
3 the encouragement given to the pupil to improvise and develop freely his own imaginative ideas.

Two useful books on this method are *Rhythm, Music and Education* by Emile Jaques-Dalcroze (Dalcroze Society, 1973) and *Rhythm and Movement* – the application of Dalcroze Eurythmics by Elsa Findlay (Summy-Birchard Company, 1834 Ridge Avenue, Evanston, Illinois 60204, USA). Further details may be obtained from the Dalcroze Society, 16 Heathcroft, Hampstead Way, London NW11 7HH.

Orff Method *Das Schulwerk* (*Music for Children*) is a creative approach to the class teaching of music, the outcome of the educational work of Carl Orff, composer and educationalist earlier this century at the Gunterschule in Munich. The basis of his teaching is rhythm which is expressed both through natural speech patterns and simple activities such as clapping and stamping. These patterns can also be sung and then played on pitched instruments like the xylophone and glockenspiel. The method is suitable for group teaching, using the differing talents and musical abilities of the children.

Orff-Schulwerk Music for Children by C. Orff and G. Keetman (Schott, 1958) explains this approach, and *Music for Children* Vols 1–5 by Carl Orff (Schott, 1951) is accompanied by gramophone records (Columbia 33 CX 1549). Schott are also the sole agents for the 'Studio 49' range of percussion instruments.

Tobin Music System This is a British method developed by Candida Tobin in the 1960s, based on visual techniques which are applied to all aspects of music teaching. Colours are used both as a means of explaining theory and identifying notes on instruments such as the recorder and guitar, and rhythm is taught using shapes to show the relationships of the various note lengths. French time names and musical shorthand are also used. All literature can be obtained from The Helicon Press, Knight Street, Sawbridgeworth, Herts CM21 9AX.

APPENDIX 2 MUSIC RESOURCES

RECORDED MUSIC

Children will listen to *short snippets* of almost any kind of music, provided it is *rhythmic* or *imaginative* and especially if *you* like it. Remember to let them hear the music you select several times fairly soon after its first introduction so that they can get to know it really well.

Suggestions for listening are given below and the symbols applied to some of the music will provide a rough guide to record selection:

* Rhythmic/exciting	Atmospheric: □ Violent/eerie
† March	○ Peaceful/pastoral
● Dancing	§ Sad

Music with a strong story line

* *Peter and the Wolf* by Prokofiev (animal theme)
● *Coppelia* by Delibes (toy theme)
* *The Sorcerer's Apprentice* by Dukas (water theme)
Hänsel and Gretel by Humperdinck
(Gingerbread Waltz, Witch's Ride, Dance Duet, Evening Prayer)
● *The Nutcracker Suite* by Tchaikovsky (toy theme)
(Chinese Dance, Dance of the Flutes, Dance of the Sugar-Plum Fairy and The Six Fairies Variations)
* *The Fire Bird* by Stravinsky
□* *Petrushka* by Stravinsky (toy theme)
(The opening fair scene music is good for a fair atmosphere.)
* *Billy the Kid* by Copland (cowboy theme)
● *La Fille Mal Gardé* by Lanchberry
(Clog dance)
The Three Bears by Eric Coates (animal theme)

Music for use with classroom themes

Toys
* *The Fantastic Toyshop* by Rossini/Respighi
Toy Symphony by Haydn
Children's Corner Suite by Debussy
○ Doll's Serenade
* Golliwog's Cakewalk
§ *The Nursery Suite* by Elgar (The Sad Doll)

• Knight of the Hobby Horse (from *Scenes of Childhood*) by Schumann
§ Dolly Suite (*Berceuse*) by Fauré
* *Jack-in-the-Box Pantomime* by Satie
• *Dancing Doll* by Poldini
Jeux d'Enfants by Bizet
1 March – trumpet and drum
2 Doll's cradle song
3 Impromptu – a whirling top
4 Duet – children
5 Gallop – a ball

Fairs and Circuses
† *The Radetsky March* by Strauss
* *The Comedians* by Kabalevsky
* The Acrobats (from *The Bartered Bride*) by Smetana
• *Circus Polka* by Stravinsky
* *Rhapsodie Espagnole* (excerpts) by Ravel
• *Clowns' Dance* by Ibert
• *Dance of the Tumblers* by Rimsky-Korsakov

Clocks
Symphony 101: *The Clock* by Haydn
The Viennese Musical Clock (from *Háry János Suite*) by Kodály
32 Pieces for Mechanical Clocks by Haydn

Space
□ *The Planets Suite* by Holst
□ Music from the film *2001* : A space odyssey
□* *Also sprach Zarathustra* (Opus 30) by Richard Strauss
□ Moving Percussion and Electronic Sound Pictures from *Listen, Move and Dance* 4 (HMV CLP 3531) (contains a journey to the moon)
Spaceships; Ghosts (sound effects) (HMV 7FX 15)

Weather and Seasons
□ *The Rite of Spring* by Stravinsky
□ *Night on the Bare Mountain* by Mussorgsky
○ The *Pastoral Symphony* by Beethoven
○ *Nocturnes* (night music) by Chopin
○ *The Four Seasons* by Vivaldi
□ The Storm from *William Tell* by Rossini
○ *A Midsummer Night's Dream* by Mendelssohn
• The snow is dancing (from *Children's Corner Suite*) by Debussy
□ *Antarctica Symphony* by Vaughan Williams

Animals

- * *Carnival of the Animals* by Saint-Saens
- ○ *The Birds:* The Hen by Respighi
- * *The Fire Bird* by Stravinsky
- ● Hatching Chicks (from *Pictures at an Exhibition*) by Mussorgsky
- ○ *The Wasps* Overture by Vaughan Williams
- ○ *Le Coucou* by Daquin
- ○ *Flight of the Bumble-bee* by Rimsky-Korsakov
- *Jungle Book* (Disney Series)
- Fun at the Zoo (BBC *Roundabout 1*) (animal sounds)
- *The Little White Donkey* by Ibert

Water

- *Noye's Fludd* by Britten
- ○ Sea Interludes (from *Peter Grimes*) by Britten
- *Water Music* by Handel
- ○ *La Mer* by Debussy
- ○ *Reflets dans l'eau* by Debussy
- ○ *The Submerged Cathedral* by Debussy
- * The Aquarium;
- ○ The Swan (from *Carnival of the Animals*) by Saint-Saëns
- * *The Flying Dutchman* Overture by Wagner
- ○ *Fingal's Cave* Overture by Mendelssohn
- *Vltava* (*Moldau*) by Smetana

Miscellaneous

- ○ *The Little Train of the Caipura* by Villa-Lobos
- * *Till Eulenspiegels* by Richard Strauss
- ● *Facade* by William Walton
- ○ *Capriol Suite* by Peter Warlock
- ○ Morning;
- * In the Hall of the Mountain King (from *Peer Gynt Suite*) by Grieg
- □ *In the Steppes of Central Asia* by Borodin
- ● *Tritsch-Tratsch Polka* by Strauss
- * *Grand Canyon Suite* by Grofé
- * *Carmen* by Bizet
- ● *The Bartered Bride* (Dances) by Smetana
- *Eine kleine Nachtmusik* by Mozart
- ● *Hungarian Dances* by Brahms
- * *Lieutenant Kije Suite* by Prokofiev
- † *Love of the Three Oranges* (the March) by Prokofiev
- * *Ride of the Valkyries* by Wagner
- ● Polka from *Schwanda the Bagpiper* by Weinberger
- ● *Les Patineurs* by Waldteufel
- ○ *The Trout Quintet* by Schubert
- * *Music for the Royal Fireworks* by Handel

Illustrating instruments

Violin	*Violin Concerto* (last movement) by Sibelius
	Alcina Minuet by Handel
Strings	Peter's theme from *Peter and the Wolf* by Prokofiev
	The Pizzicati Polka from *Sylvia* by Délibes
Cello	The Swan from *Carnival of the Animals* by Saint-Saëns
Double Bass	The Elephant from *Carnival of the Animals* by Saint-Saëns
Flute	The Bird from *Peter and the Wolf* by Prokofiev
	L'apres-midi d'une faune by Debussy
	Blue Bird Dance (2) from *The Nutcracker Suite* by Tchaikovsky
(and piccolo)	Chinese Dance from *The Nutcracker Suite* by Tchaikovsky
Oboe	The Duck from *Peter and the Wolf* by Prokofiev
	The Lilac Fairy; The Two Cats from *The Nutcracker Suite* by Tchaikovsky
(and clarinet)	Fairy of the Enchanted Garden from *The Nutcracker Suite* by Tchaikovsky
Clarinet	The Cat from *Peter and the Wolf* by Prokofiev
	Clarinet Concerto (K.622) by Mozart
	Puss in Boots from *The Nutcracker Suite* by Tchaikovsky
Bassoon	Grandfather from *Peter and the Wolf* by Prokofiev
	The Sorcerer's Apprentice by Dukas
(and oboe)	Fairy of the Crystal Fountain from *The Nutcracker Suite* by Tchaikovsky
Trumpet	*Trumpet Voluntary* by Clarke
(and flute)	Dance of the Flutes from *The Nutcracker Suite* by Tchaikovsky
	Herb Alpert and the Tijuana Brass
	Solo from *Royal Fireworks* Minuet by Handel
Trombone	*Tannhäuser* Overture by Wagner
	Pulcinella by Stravinsky
French Horn	The Wolf from *Peter and the Wolf* by Prokofiev
	Horn Concerto No. 2 (Rondo) by Mozart
Tuba	*Tubby the Tuba* by George Kleinsinger and Paul Tripp
	Tubby at the Circus by George Kleinsinger and Paul Tripp
Tenor Tuba	Bydlo from *Pictures at an Exhibition* by Mussorgsky
Xylophone	Fossils from *Carnival of the Animals* by Saint-Saëns
Celesta	Dance of the Sugar-plum Fairy from *The Nutcracker Suite* by Tchaikovsky
Castanets	*España* by Chabrier
Glockenspiel	Little Bells from *Wand of Youth Suite* No. 2 by Elgar
Classical Guitar	Any recordings by Segovia, John Williams or Julian Bream

General recordings	*Instruments of the Orchestra* commentary by Yehudi Menuhin (1977) available with a booklet from Oxford University Press

Listening
Carnival of the Animals by Saint-Saëns
(and see under 'Animals' in the Recorded Music Section of Appendix 2)

Machines

Sound picture
Machines at home: encourage as many children as possible to record the sounds of machines at home; do it yourself. Bring the tape to class for a guessing game. Find *sound words* and *sound makers* to match each machine:

Typewriter	*ticker, ticker, ticker, ch!*	trill a 'clamped' triangle and 'ping' it
Telephone	*br-br . . . br-br . . . br-br . . .*	corrugated tin, bottle or guiro
Egg whisk	*whirrr, whirrr, whirrr . . .*	rolled shaker (loud one) or a whisk itself!
Lawnmower	*errrrr-rr; errrrr-rr . . .*	washboard

Divide into four groups: encourage each group to establish a specific *rhythm*; practise these rhythms quick, slow, loud, quiet, high, low (if with the voice). Try the arrangement shown on the chart below, first with voices and then sound makers in as many different ways as possible:

(to the tune of 'The wheels on the bus'[4])

1 My typewriter goes ticker, ticker, ch! . . . all day long.
2 Our telephone goes br-br . . . br-br . . .
3 Mummy's egg whisk goes whirrr, whirrr, whirrr . . .
4 Daddy's lawnmower goes errrrrr-rr, errrrrr-rr . . .

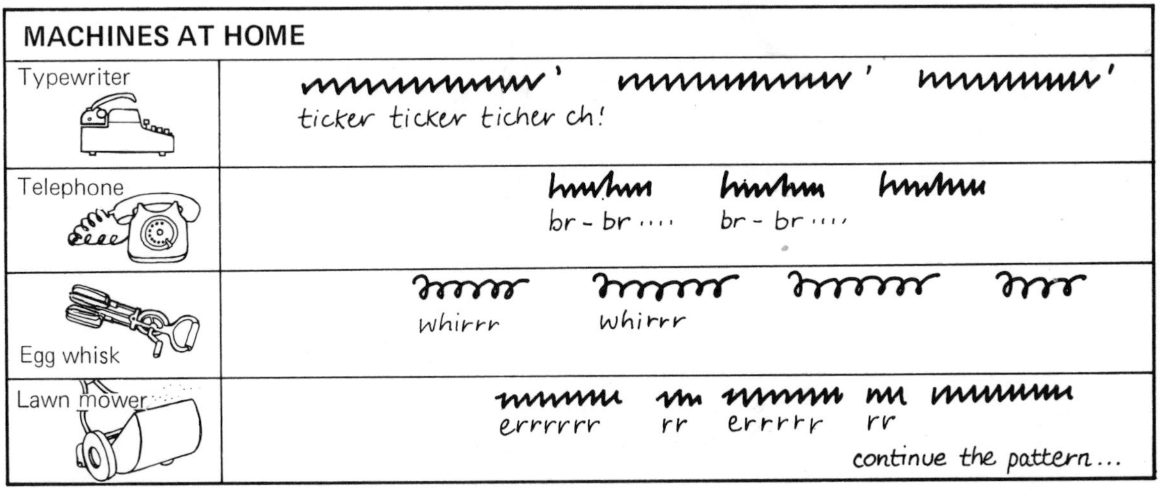

MACHINES AT HOME	
Typewriter	ticker ticker ticher ch!
Telephone	br - br .... br - br ....
Egg whisk	whirrr whirrr
Lawn mower	errrrr rr errrrr rr continue the pattern...

Poem

Creation
The dainty old professor
Made a new machine
He built it up with dead corkscrews
And junk you've never seen,
He tied it up with chewing gum
And glued it down with strings
Then watered it with fish's milk
And many other things.
He turned it on at midnight
As the sun gained height;
He was deafened by a flash
And calmly got a fright.
The thing took down the pictures
And ironed them with a broom;
Sang 'Greensleeves' in a rusty voice
And flew about the room.

It fed the fire with stuffing
From the lounge settee;
It washed the cakes and cooked the clothes
With great alacrity.
It ate the wine and read the bread
And drank the 'Herald' dry;
It nailed some biscuits onto toast
And quietly drowned a pie.

It knocked the clock from the mantelpiece
And put some ham instead;
It sewed some tissue paper up
With cotton wire and thread.
It swept the floor with rolling pin
And brushed the lawn for fleas;
It sawed some wood with plastic comb
And climbed up all the trees.

It makes a lovely housewife, its hair is turning grey,
He wouldn't want another, in case it passed away.
Graeme Turner

Songs
Machines[35]
Wheels keep turning[1]
This is the sound our Hoover makes (to the tune of 'Mulberry Bush')

Stories

Mary Poppins in the Kitchen by P.J. Traves (Collins)
Ben in the Kitchen by Pat Albeck (Methuen)
Barbamama's Kitchen by Talus Taylor and Annette Tison (Warne)

Listening

Moving Percussion and Electronic Sound Pictures (*Listen, Move and Dance* No. 4, HMV/CLP/3531)
Perpetuum Mobile by Johann Strauss

SOUND EXPERIMENTS

Noise

I like noise.
The whoop of a boy, the thud of a hoof,
The rattle of rain on a galvanised roof,
The hubbub of traffic, the roar of a train,
The throb of machinery numbing the brain,
The switching of wires in an overhead tram,
The rush of the wind, the door on the slam,
The boom of thunder, the crash of the waves,
The din of a river that races and raves,
The crack of a rifle, the clank of a pail,
The strident tattoo of a swift-slapping sail –
From any old sound that the silence destroys
Arises a gamut of soul-stirring joys.
I like noise.
J. Pope

The nature of sound

This section outlines some basic knowledge that is helpful to have in mind when talking about sound with children, and there are a few simple experiments which the children might do. Always try out experiments yourself first so that you know they will work.

Little children will be absorbed mainly in their own efforts at *making sound*; they will be fascinated by the range of sound they can produce from the various kinds of material they can lay their hands on and they will try out different rhythms and sound effects.

1. Focus on sounds through the listening games and music-corner activities already suggested.
2. Provide for the making of some simple percussion instruments; the children will learn a lot about the properties of sound through handling the material.
3. Make some shoebox animals that roar!

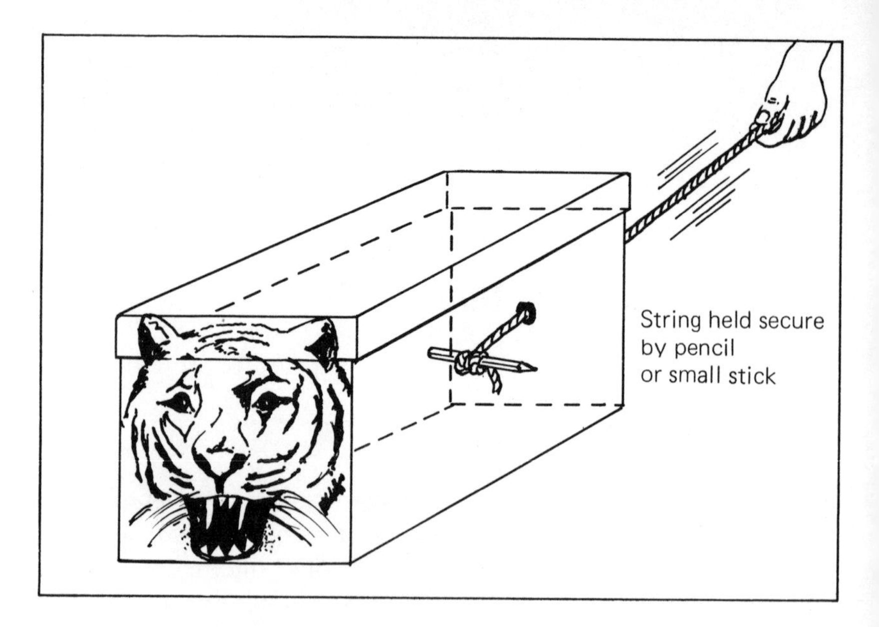

Run some chalk on the string and pull along the tail with finger and thumb. Paint a face on the front to suit the 'roar'. Try different-sized boxes and types of string.

4 Make a toy stethoscope – try listening to a watch ticking.

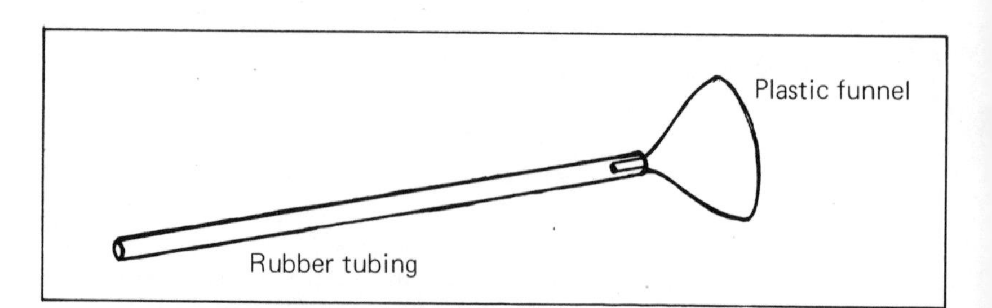

5 Try to get hold of a real stethoscope for listening to body sounds.

6 Make a megaphone out of strong card. How does it change the children's voices?

7 How else can we affect the way we hear sound?
 (a) Put hands over ears.
 (b) Put cotton wool in ears (nothing should ever be *poked* into ears).
 (c) Turn on a small transistor radio or cassette player and put it into a shoebox filled with material or a duster.

Can the children think of any other ways of muffling sound?

8 Discuss people's voices: some are deep; some are gruff; children have high-pitched voices; some babies cry a lot. Voices are used for laughing, crying, talking, shouting, cheering; they show feeling.

9 Animals make sounds of their own: how do they use them? They have different shaped ears: how does the size of their ears help them? Try cupping hands around ears. Fish are said to make sounds that are inaudible to humans.
10 Sounds in the environment have meanings – for example those produced by the telephone, alarm clock, whistling kettle, a car's horn, an ambulance.

Ways of producing sound

When the children have had plenty of experience of making sounds by themselves, examine with them the various ways they had found of producing those sounds. They will fall roughly into these categories which are the basic groupings that can apply to musical instruments:

Percussion:	*banging* – hitting, tapping, striking – virtually anything within reason
	shaking – rattle, a pencil box, head of hair, wind chimes (gently)
Wind instruments:	*blowing* – a whistle, kazoo, recorder, across the top of a bottle, mouth organ.
Stringed instruments:	*rubbing* – hands, sand-block, hands on clothes or different materials, scrubbing brush. Drawing a violin bow across the strings is a rubbing action.
	twanging – a rubber-band stretched over a box, a ruler, a guitar string.

Once through this exploratory stage, the children's natural curiosity in how things work will lead them on to try a few simple experiments.

What causes a sound?

Sound is caused by a *vibration* – a new word that will take on meaning with a few experiments.

1 The children can feel the vibration:
(a) Let them put their fingers on their throats when they speak or sing; they can also feel a cat purring.
(b) Let them feel the buzzing of tissue paper on their lips when they blow through a comb.
(c) Let them gently feel the vibrating end of a tuning fork that has just been struck, with their tongues or fingertips.
(d) Let them lightly touch a violin or guitar string that is being played, or the loudspeaker of a radio or tape recorder that is playing.

2 The children can see the vibration:
   (a) Let them sprinkle some seeds or sand onto a drumhead and watch them bounce when the drum is played.
   (b) Let them strike a tuning fork and put the vibrating end into some water or touch a suspended table-tennis ball.
   (c) Let them twang a rubber-band stretched over a box.

3 They can hear the sound!
   As you might expect, the *bigger* the vibration the *louder* the sound. The children can:
   (a) sprinkle some seeds or sand onto a drumhead and observe the change in the size of the bounce when the drum is played loudly, then very quietly;
   (b) twang a stretched rubber-band energetically, then gently, and observe the difference in the size of the movement and the sound;
   (c) do the same experiment by flipping the end of a ruler or nailfile projecting over the edge of a table;
   (d) similarly twang a guitar string;
   (e) drop a large stone, then a small stone, into a basin or pond (the water must be still) and compare the sound of the plops and the size of the ripples.

Pitch The pitch of a sound is determined by the rate of the vibration or 'frequency'; the *faster* or greater the frequency of the vibration, the *higher* the sound. Thus middle A – the note on which orchestras tune up – corresponds to a frequency of 440 vibrations per second. The lowest note on a piano has a frequency of about 25 vibrations per second and the highest note about 3,500. A *percussion sound* (drum, cymbal, shaker, etc.) doesn't seem to have a definite pitch because it is made up of a *jumble of frequencies.* (The technical way of saying so many 'vibrations per second' is so many 'cycles per second' or so many 'hertz', sometimes abbreviated to 'Hz'.)

Because the frequency of even the lowest note that can be heard (about 16 hertz) is so high, you cannot demonstrate visually the relation between pitch and rate of vibration. However you can show that when a vibrator is *shortened*, the pitch *rises* (and vice versa):

1 Pluck any guitar string: let the children hear the change in pitch as you move your finger up the string stopping each fret, and thus shortening the length of the vibrator.
2 Cover all the holes of a descant recorder, lift up the fingers one by one starting from the bottom; the children will hear the pitch rising as you blow for each note until finally all the holes are uncovered and one of the highest notes is heard.

The vibrator is the column of air inside the recorder; this is shortened as the holes are uncovered.

3 Arrange some chimebars in order of size; compare the sounds, playing from one end of the group to the other. The vibrator is the white metal part.
4 Play up and down a xylophone and a glockenspiel.
5 Blow across an empty medicine bottle; partly fill it with water and blow again. Continue until it is filled with water. The vibrator is the column of air inside (tapping gives a different result).

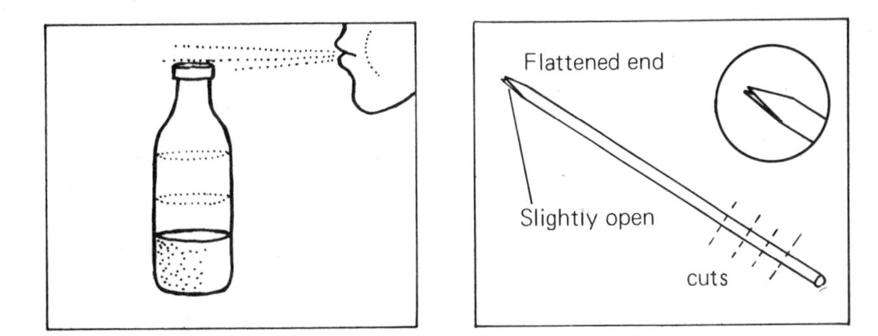

6 Show the children how to make a milk-straw pipe. Flatten and trim one end of a waxed (non-plastic) straw: blow into the cut end to get a squawk or 'raspberry'. Continue blowing but keep cutting off bits from the far end of the straw; the children will hear the pitch of the squawk rise. The vibrator is the column of air inside the straw.

The pitch of a vibrating string depends not only on its *length* but also on its *tension* and the *material from which it is made*:

1 Tighten a guitar string and listen to the pitch rise.
2 Feel the difference between the highest and lowest strings.
3 Take the front off a piano and observe the differences in the strings as you play high and low notes.

Quality The same note has a different *quality* or *character* when played on different types of instrument. This is because when a note is played on a musical instrument, higher notes are also produced which have frequencies double or treble the note played; these are called overtones or harmonics. It is the *mixture of overtones* that we hear when a single note is played that gives it its quality. Because the relative strengths of the overtones vary with the instrument, each instrument has its own distinctive quality or timbre. A tuning fork does not produce overtones, hence its 'pure' sound. A rich sound is made up of many overtones. Very high notes seem thin because the overtones are beyond our limits of hearing.

How sound travels

What is actually happening when you hear a chimebar? Air is made up of millions of very small particles of gases. When tapped, the chimebar vibrates and this makes the gas particles in contact with it vibrate at the same rate. The vibrations are then transferred to other particles slightly further away from the bar and multiple collisions continue until the particles nearest to the ear press against the diaphragm, causing it to vibrate as well. A message goes up the nerves to the brain which registers that it hears a sound corresponding to that rate of vibration.

Through air

Sound travels through air at a speed of about one mile every five seconds.

1 Observe with the children someone hammering in the distance. They will notice that they *see* each stroke before they *hear* it because light travels much faster than sound.
2 You can tell how far away a thunderstorm is by counting in seconds from the moment of the lightning flash until the first peal of thunder. Divide by five to get the distance in miles.

Through solids and liquids

Sound travels through solids and liquids as well. The most obvious illustration is that sounds are continually coming into our classrooms from outside (even with the windows shut!), but here are some specific experiments:

Wood

1 Lay a ticking wristwatch down on one end of a wooden table, or desk. Listen in at the other end, with one ear touching the table.
2 Listen in while a friend taps the table with a pencil. Then listen with ears off the table and compare the sound of the taps.

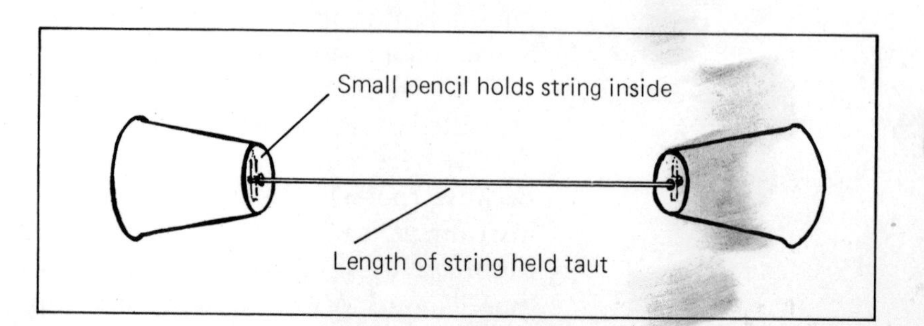